After Disaster

American Governance and Public Policy

A SERIES EDITED BY

Barry Rabe and John Tierney

This series examines a broad range of public policy issues and their relationship to all levels of government in the United States. The editors welcome serious scholarly studies and seek to publish books that appeal to both academic and professional audiences. The series showcases studies that illuminate the successes, as well as the problems, of policy formulation and implementation.

After Disaster

Agenda Setting, Public Policy, and Focusing Events

Thomas A. Birkland

GEORGETOWN UNIVERSITY PRESS / WASHINGTON, D.C.

Georgetown University Press, Washington, D.C. 20007
© 1997 by Georgetown University Press. All rights reserved.

10 9 8 7 6 5 4 3 2 1   1997

THIS VOLUME IS PRINTED ON ACID-FREE ⊗ OFFSET BOOK PAPER

Library of Congress Cataloging-in-Publication Data

Birkland, Thomas A.
    After disaster : agenda setting, public policy, and focusing
events / Thomas A. Birkland.
        p.   cm.—(American governance and public policy)
    Includes bibliographical references and index.
    1. Political planning—United States. 2. Policy sciences.
3. Natural disasters—Government policy—United States. 4. Oil
spills—Government policy—United States. 5. Nuclear power plants—
Accidents—Government policy—United States.   I. Title.
II. Series.
JK468.P64B57   1997
320′.6—DC21   97-7908
ISBN 0-87840-652-2
ISBN 0-87840-653-0 (pbk.)

Contents

List of Selected Abbreviations

ACF   Advocacy Coalition Framework
AEC   Atomic Energy Commission, predecessor of the NRC
ANILCA   Alaska National Interest Lands Conservation Act
ANWR   Arctic National Wildlife Refuge
AOR   Abnormal Occurrence Report
CNI   Consolidated National Intervenors
CWA   Clean Water Act
DOE   Department of Energy
DWPA   Deepwater Port Act of 1974
ECCS   Emergency Core Cooling System
EERI   Earthquake Engineering Research Institute
EPA   Environmental Protection Agency
ERDA   Energy Research and Development Agency
FAA   Federal Aviation Administration
FEMA   Federal Emergency Management Agency
FOE   Friends of the Earth
FWPCA   Federal Water Pollution Control Act (later known as the Clean Water Act [CWA])
GOO   Get Oil Out, a post-Santa Barbara oil spill advocacy group
JCAE   Joint Committee on Atomic Energy
LILCO   Long Island Lighting Company
MMS   Minerals Management Service (Department of Interior)
NEHRA   National Earthquake Hazards Reduction Act
NEHRP   National Earthquake Hazards Reduction Program
NEPA   National Environmental Policy Act
NFIP   National Flood Insurance Program
NRC   Nuclear Regulatory Commission
NRDC   Natural Resources Defense Council
NTSB   National Transportation Safety Board

OLS	Ordinary least squares (regression method)
OPA	Oil Pollution Act of 1990
TAPAA	Trans-Alaska Pipeline Authorization Act
TAPS	Trans-Alaska Pipeline System
TAP	Trans-Alaska Pipeline
TMI	Three Mile Island nuclear power plant
TVA	Tennessee Valley Authority
UCS	Union of Concerned Scientists

Preface

Sudden disasters and catastrophes are important events in our individual lives and in the collective memory of the nation. At some point in our lives, we can expect to be directly or indirectly touched by a natural disaster or by a major industrial or technological accident. Those of us with family or friends who have been victimized by disasters or accidents vividly remember these catastrophes, our worry for their well-being, and our awe when told of their sometimes harrowing experiences. We endure, or learn from family and friends, fears of danger and economic loss after industrial accidents. We experience or hear of the loss of one's livelihood, or the sorrow and anger that comes with the fouling of a pristine wilderness. Many events—the *Exxon Valdez* oil spill, Three Mile Island, the Loma Prieta Earthquake, Hurricane Hugo—by their mere names conjure vivid and indelible images of destruction, fear, and environmental degradation. For many of us, these events often serve as shared social and political experiences in which we ask each other, "Do you remember where you were when . . . ?"

Sudden and vivid events are important to me because one such event—the *Exxon Valdez* oil spill in 1989—led me to ask the questions that I consider in this book. I grew up in Alaska and knew many of the places where spilled oil washed ashore. I knew people who worked on the cleanup of the spill and who studied its aftermath. My years in Alaska gave me a sense of how Alaskans, in particular, would react to this sudden, shocking, and in many ways heartbreaking catastrophe. Later we learned that, while the spill was in some ways an environmental disaster, the most dire predictions of the long-term effects of oil on the ecosystem may not come to pass. Still, Alaskans—and many other Americans—viewed the images of oiled beaches and sea creatures and found themselves torn between their desire to promote economic growth and access to domestic oil and to their desire to protect the environment against seemingly reckless corporations. The *Exxon Valdez* spill threw this dilemma—that has been important in American politics for years and in Alaska since before its statehood—into the starkest relief since the Santa Barbara oil spill of 1969.

This apparent similarity between the *Exxon Valdez* spill and the 1969 Santa Barbara spill led me to wonder what it was about these events that make them important in the policy-making process. This question was further animated by the number of times one can find references by students of the policy process, usually in passing, to the importance of events in public policy making. Most prominent among these scholars is John Kingdon. In his landmark book *Agendas, Alternatives and Public Policies* (1995), Kingdon described *focusing events* that cause many people—bureaucrats, elected officials, and the general public—to pay greater attention to the problems revealed by these events. Other students of the policy process—Cobb and Elder (1983), Baumgartner and Jones (1993) and Light (1982)—also cite the importance of sudden, vivid events in stimulating greater interest in a problem and possibly inducing policy change. But for all the mentions of this phenomenon in the policy-making and agenda-setting literature, there has been little theoretical or empirical research that explores how such events influence the policy process. In this book, I hope to close this gap.

*   *   *

It is said that writing a book is a supremely solitary act, but this book, like most others, is also the product of fruitful conversations and collaborations with many people. Their help and encouragement make this book much stronger than it would otherwise be. Indeed, without some of the people who have challenged me to extend and clarify this argument, the book would not have been possible at all. Of course, I remain responsible for any gaps between their able assistance and the results of this study.

The research that formed the foundation of this study was supported by the Federal Emergency Management Agency (FEMA) and the Earthquake Engineering Research Institute (EERI). These organizations award the National Earthquake Hazards Reduction Program (NEHRP)/EERI graduate fellowship, and I am grateful for being selected as their 1993–1994 graduate fellow. Susan Tubbesing and the EERI staff were particularly helpful in providing information, and I thank the Institute for inviting me to present preliminary results of this study at their 1995 meeting in San Francisco. I am also grateful to the University of Washington Graduate School for their award of a dissertation grant.

At the University of Washington, Peter May was instrumental in helping me advance these ideas from the realm of intuition or guesswork to a more rigorously theoretical discussion that could inform, and be informed by, empirical analysis. Paul Burstein, David Olson, and Stuart Scheingold were patient and persistent critics, and their ideas and suggestions significantly improved this work.

A particular debt is owed to my colleagues at the University of Washington, who, as part of our informal reading group, were exceedingly generous in sharing ideas and criticism. Karen Anderson, Mike Bollom, Shane Fricks, Regina Lawrence, Sheila Rucki, and Rich Sherman were meticulous in their reviews of early versions of this book, much to my ultimate benefit (even if it didn't feel like it at the time). Regina Lawrence, Mark Donovan, and Judy Aks read the penultimate draft, and their close reading and rereading helped sharpen the argument and reveal lapses in logic that deserved correction. At the University at Albany, Scott Barclay, Tom Church, Ben Fordham, and Bob Nakamura have also provided their comments and suggestions. Ben has been particularly patient in helping me untie some methodological knots.

I thank John Samples of Georgetown University Press, the series editors, John Tierney and Barry Rabe, and anonymous reviewers for their patience in working with a newcomer to the world of academic publishing. John Samples has been particularly helpful in patiently explaining the ins and outs of academic publishing.

I dedicate this book to my parents, James and Kathleen Birkland. I was fortunate to write the earliest versions of this book "back home" in Seattle, and my parents provided a much-needed refuge from the rigors of writing and rewriting. Very early in this project, my mother volunteered to do most of the rather tedious data entry work, wearing out at least two keyboards in the process of entering data that became four large databases. I am grateful for her help, and for the emotional and material encouragement both of them gave me to pursue my academic interests in public policy making.

1

Focusing Events, Agenda Setting, and the Policy Process

This book is about how sudden, unpredictable events called *focusing events* influence the public policy-making process. I develop a theory of focusing events by employing a rich variety of literature on the policy process, including agenda setting, group competition, the political aspects of the news media, and the use of symbols in political debate. In so doing, I analyze data spanning one to three decades of policy-making activity dealing with natural disasters, oil spills, and nuclear power plant accidents.

While focusing events are often an important part of policy making, I make no claim that focusing events are always important or are the sole trigger of attention to a problem. Other scholars have studied the role of social and economic change in politics and policy. Political crisis, rather than being the result of a single event or a handful of events, may often result from a period of inexorable social change and conflict. The expansion of government in the New Deal era, for example, was the result of long-term social change and growing demands for government to mitigate downturns in the business cycle. Health insurance reform has waxed and waned fairly regularly on the agenda, at least since the Truman administration. These issues, and others like them, come and go as their underlying political, economic, and demographic elements change. Problems and proposed solutions move higher and lower on the agenda as a result of conflicting interpretations of facts and trends and with changes in the ideological tastes of the electorate. More "liberal" electoral trends lead to periods of more extensive governmental activity, while more "conservative" periods lead, per to a retrenchment of government and, perhaps, to a reduction in the number of tasks government undertakes. These trends may take years to be recognized and even longer to have an influence on policy making, and in these cases it is difficult to identify one or a few points in time as critical in the life cycles of these issues.

1

Whereas long-term social change is often the result of the ebb and flow of broader social and economic conditions, social change and conflict are often punctuated by sharp, sudden events. But while a focusing event can be a much more rapid and easily identifiable impetus for policy-making activity and potential policy change, the dynamics of such events have not yet been systematically explained. The environmental movement, for example, grew in prominence throughout the 1960s, as indicators of the extent of environmental degradation were revealed in books, magazines, and government reports. The growth of environmentalism, based on this increasing awareness of environmental damage, was rapidly and dramatically accelerated by highly visible environmental catastrophes such as the 1969 Santa Barbara oil spill. Similarly, the expansion of the civil rights movement can be attributed to a slowly building social movement inching toward broader support for racial equality, punctuated with sudden, highly visible manifestations of the meaning and importance of the movement (Carmines and Stimson 1989). These events include the 1963 March on Washington, which featured Martin Luther King's "I Have A Dream" speech, and the use of police dogs and fire hoses on civil rights marchers in Birmingham, Alabama.

These examples illustrate how familiar these events, or others like them, are to most of us. Many of us can remember exactly where we were, and what we were doing, when such events became widely known, and our individual and collective responses to these events tend to follow similar patterns, regardless of the specifics of the event. A large event occurs—an oil spill, a plane crash, or a natural disaster—and the news media converge on the scene of the accident or disaster. Dramatic footage is aired and photographs are printed of property damage, visible environmental damage, homeless victims, and grieving families. Soon thereafter, the media's attention (and our own) turns to people who can explain why the event happened: corporate officers, government officials, experts, and community leaders. When society seems to have formed a consensus that the event was an "act of God," such as a natural disaster or freak accident, our attention turns to what we can do to help the victims. But when the disaster is the result of human failings—poor design, operator error, "corporate greed," or "government neglect"—our attention turns to the voluntary acceptance of responsibility for an event or to the more coercive process of fixing blame. Boards of inquiry are formed, legislatures hold hearings, and reports are issued, all in hopes of "learning something from this incident" to ensure that something similar does not happen again or, in the case of "unavoidable" disasters, in hopes of improving our preparation for and response to disasters. These are familiar outcomes. The question I pose is: How does this activity influence the policy process? I start by considering the role of focusing events in agenda setting.

FOCUSING EVENTS AS AN ELEMENT OF AGENDA SETTING

This book is primarily a study of a particular and previously unexplored element of the agenda. A more detailed theory of focusing events, which I apply to case studies in chapters 3, 4, and 5, is outlined in detail in chapter 2. In this chapter I outline the theoretical foundations on which the theory of focusing events is built. To preview, a *potential focusing event* (that is, an event than can be, but is not necessarily, focusing) is a rare, harmful, sudden event that becomes known to the mass public and policy elites virtually simultaneously. The agenda-setting power of these events derives from these features. In the models of focusing events that follow, these features suggest variables that influence the agenda-setting power of the event. Current thinking on agenda setting provides the foundation for the creation of these models.

There are at least three reasons to improve our understanding of focusing events as factors in agenda setting. The first reason is that this is intuitively sensible. On nearly any day it is relatively simple to find examples of events that caused individuals or society at large to ask why the problem had not been considered before and what ought to be done about it. For example, in 1993 one might run across a news story like this: a natural gas pipeline exploded near an apartment development in Edison, New Jersey. The incident led the state to enact rules requiring contractors to notify residents before digging near pipelines (New York Times 1994). Quite sensibly, this event caused people to take note of, examine, and, in this case, do something about the problem—excavation near gas pipelines—revealed by the event. Without the accident it is unlikely that any *notice* of this problem, regardless of its likelihood or potential for disaster, would have occurred. The issue was destined to remain low on the agenda, with legislation unlikely, until the accident occurred.

The *Exxon Valdez* oil spill, a prominent example in this book, is a more widely known event that led to policy change. As I show in chapter 4, the Oil Pollution Act of 1990 was passed largely in reaction to the *Exxon Valdez* oil spill. Without the *Exxon Valdez* spill, it is more likely that a fourteen-year-long legislative deadlock over comprehensive oil spill liability legislation would have persisted, and any policy change would have languished, probably until some other huge oil spill came to dominate the agenda and dramatize the problem. Again, a focusing event will not necessarily equal policy change, but can be an important precursor under certain circumstances. I more fully describe how focusing events can contribute to policy change in chapter 6.

A second reason to improve our understanding of focusing events is to close an important gap in the study of agenda setting and policy making. While focusing events are often cited as important by policy scholars, there is little systematic research on how and why these events are important. Kingdon discusses the phenomenon at great length because his informants cite focusing events as important in driving agenda change. Cobb and Elder examine events they call "circumstantial reactors," such as "the development of an oil slick off the California coast near Santa Barbara in 1969 that led to a reconsideration of the whole question of offshore drilling regulations" (Cobb and Elder 1983, 83). Circumstantial reactors include natural disasters and human events, such as riots, assassinations, and hijackings. Broader ecological change, such as population growth, economic shifts, and black migration, are also a form of circumstantial reactors, but the onset of these factors is much more subtle than natural disasters or technological accidents and is therefore less likely to serve as a time-definite rallying point for group attention and mobilization. As Kingdon argues, subtle changes are less likely to be viewed as "events" than are sudden, dramatic, and visible problems.

These definitions of focusing events are suggestive but are underdeveloped in the broader theories in which they are introduced. Considering the apparent importance of focusing events in the policy process and agenda-setting literature, it is important more fully to specify a theory of how focusing events are "focal." If such events are relatively unimportant or have random or idiosyncratic agenda-setting effects that can be isolated from other factors, then their influence on the agenda, as hypothesized by these theorists, may be overstated. Whatever the case, this is an important gap in our knowledge that is worth narrowing.

A third reason for studying focusing events is that the tentative definitions of focusing events provided in current research suggest a theory that can be studied empirically. Such a study is made possible by the availability of a considerable amount of information—contained in readily available public records—that reflects the dynamics of the agenda-setting process. The influence of a particular event should be detectable because focusing events are much easier to pinpoint as proximate causes of agenda change at a particular moment than are social, demographic, or ideological changes. This is not to say that focusing events are the sole or even the most important cause of agenda change in any particular domain. But, for those domains in which focusing events are important, this feature of focusing events makes studying their influence relatively straightforward and supports calls for more empirical studies of policy-making phenomena.

AGENDA SETTING AND THE STUDY OF PUBLIC POLICY

Any study of agenda setting—the process by which issues gain greater mass and elite attention—is about the policy process broadly and about the politics of policy subsystems in particular (Baumgartner and Jones 1993, 43). Thinking of these elements of the policy process as being intertwined prevents us from succumbing to the analytical shortcomings of what became called the "stages" model of policy making (Sabatier 1988). During the primacy of this heuristic, studies of policy making tended to focus on disparate or discrete policy areas. Such studies assumed that policy making proceeds in a relatively orderly, step-wise fashion, beginning with problem identification and agenda setting, and ending with policy implementation and feedback. While this approach is still a staple of many undergraduate public policy textbooks, Greenberg et al. (1977) argued twenty years ago that the proliferation of empirically untested theories created a need for synthesis and testing of the explicit and implicit hypotheses raised by these studies. Echoing and extending this call for greater theoretical rigor, Sabatier (1991) argued that studies of the policy process should move beyond simple statements and restatements of theory. Better theories should synthesize existing theory, should transcend the compartmentalization of the stages heuristic, and should more consciously seek to specify causal mechanisms. In short, better theories of the policy process must avoid the tendency to arrange policy making into neat, orderly steps.

Dissatisfaction with the stages heuristic, and its replacement with improved metaphors or models of the policy process, does not deny the utility of *labeling* particular elements of the process using the nomenclature of the stages heuristic. After all, as a way of helping us to organize our thinking about the policy process, the stages model works well; it is just too linear and deterministic to serve as policy *theory*. Thus, we can consider problem definition, agenda setting, policy adoption, and implementation as categories of activities in ongoing policy competition that, taken together, help us to understand the policy process. These activities take place constantly, often overlap, and may often lead to dead ends (greater agenda status failing to "lead" to policy change, for example).

Modern Models of the Policy Process

In this book, I rely extensively on two current models of the policy process: John Kingdon's "streams" metaphor of the policy process and Paul Sabatier's Advocacy Coalition Framework (ACF).

John Kingdon argues that issues gain agenda status, and alternative solutions are selected, when elements of three "streams" come together. Each of these three streams contains various individuals, groups, agencies, and institutions that are involved in the policy-making process. One stream encompasses the state of politics and public opinion (the *political stream*). A second stream contains the potential solutions to a problem (the *policy stream*). The third, the *problem stream*, encompasses the attributes of a problem and whether it is getting better or worse, whether it has suddenly sprung into public and elite consciousness through a focusing event, and whether it is solvable with the alternatives available in the policy stream. Within any one problem area, these streams run parallel and somewhat independently of each other in a policy area or domain until something happens to cause the streams to meet in a "window of opportunity." This window is the possibility of policy change, but the opening of the window does not guarantee that policy change will occur. That trigger can be a change in our understanding of the problem, a change in the political stream that is favorable to policy change, a change in our understanding of the tractability of the problem given current solutions, or a focusing event that draws attention to a problem and helps open a window of opportunity.

Sabatier (1991) argues that the streams metaphor may be an incomplete description of policy making because it does not describe the policy process beyond the opening of the window of opportunity. In contrast, Zahariadis (1993) argues that the streams approach can be applied to decision opportunities, not simply agenda-setting opportunities; a *decision* to make new or change existing policy may be more likely when the streams come together. Thus, Kingdon provides a rich and multilayered metaphor of policy making from the early acceptance of new ideas about public problems to the active considerations of solutions as new public policy. Kingdon's metaphor is important to my thinking about focusing events because he introduces the idea of focusing events in a much clearer way than prior policy theory. The three streams thus suggest different types of event variables that can be examined for their influence on the agenda.

Sabatier's Advocacy Coalition Framework (ACF) is important to this study because it is predicated on the idea that policy communities organize within a policy domain. This study begins with this assumption to study how events influence policy making and politics in these policy domains and communities. The term "policy domain" is further defined and discussed in terms of its relationship to a policy "community" later in this chapter. In the ACF, two to four advocacy coalitions typically form in a particular policy domain when groups coalesce around a shared set of core values and beliefs. These groups engage in policy debate, and compete and compromise on solutions based on their core values and beliefs. Competition between coalitions is mediated by policy brokers who have a stake in resolving the problem, either on substantive grounds or because of their interest in maintaining political harmony in the system. These brokers are more likely to succeed when they can develop compromises that do not threaten either advocacy coalition's core beliefs and values. Policy change is much less likely if polarization of advocacy coalitions is so great that there is no room in the periphery of the groups' belief systems in which compromise can be found. Like the streams metaphor, Sabatier's ACF encompasses a variety of individual and institutional actors, and it views policy making as an iterative process that runs over years or decades. The ACF also considers the mechanisms for policy change (not simply the possibility for change, as in the streams metaphor) and more consciously encompasses the influence of implementation and feedback on the system.

In the ACF, policy making is influenced both by "relatively stable" system parameters and by "dynamic (system) events," with the interaction between the two promoting or inhibiting policy making. The stable parameters include the basic attributes of the problem area, the basic distribution of natural resources in the society, the fundamental cultural values and social structure, and the basic legal structure, which in the United States is the constitutional framework and judicial norms. The dynamic features of the system include changes in socioeconomic conditions and technology, changes in systemic governing coalitions (partisan balance in the legislature or the executive branch, for example), and policy decisions and impacts from other subsystems. Change in the governing coalition corresponds to one example of change in the political stream in Kingdon's model, while changes in socioeconomic and technological conditions influence the problem and policy streams. The activities of other subsystems can influence the policy, politics, and problems streams as their activities spill over into other policy domains.

If we understand agenda setting as an important element of group competition, the importance of this idea, and of studies devoted to understanding agenda setting in particular contexts, becomes much clearer. For example, Walker studied agenda setting in the U.S. Senate, finding that "the agenda is determined by forces outside the control of the members" (1977, 423). Similarly, Light (1982) studied how the president controls, or is controlled by, the agenda. Light found that the president must establish his agenda early and must seek action on his priorities before electoral pressures or unforeseen events or crises drive his agenda. This effect is very likely to be negative from the executive's perspective unless the president and his staff can either substantively or symbolically address the crisis, but these events can be positive if they provide the impetus to advance a pet element of the president's agenda. These studies help us to understand how institutional actors participate in policy making more generally, not simply in agenda setting considered in a vacuum. My study extends the foundation laid by these scholars by specifying the features of these events that cause them to attract mass and elite attention, or, in other words, to be more "focal."

Agenda Setting as a Key Activity in Policy Making

In *The Semi-Sovereign People*, E.E. Schattschneider asserted that "the definition of the alternatives is the supreme instrument of power" (1960/1975, 66). The definition of alternative issues, problems, and solutions is crucial, for it establishes which issues, problems, and solutions will or will not be addressed by mass publics and decision makers. Agenda setting is the process by which problems and alternative solutions gain or lose public and elite attention. This is a crucial activity, since few, if any, societies have the institutional capacity to address all possible alternatives to all possible problems that arise at any one time (Hilgartner and Bosk 1988).

Since Schattschneider's day, several strands of agenda-setting theory have developed, all of which are predicated on the idea that there are several layers of the agenda. Many problems, ideas, and solutions can be elevated from obscurity to intense public and policy-making interest, or fade again as other issues become more important. In this book I concentrate on the influence of focusing events on the federal institutional agenda overall and the legislative branch in particular.

Central to understanding agenda setting is the meaning of the term *agenda*. An agenda is a collection of problems, understandings of causes, symbols, solutions, and other elements of public problems that come to the attention of members of the public and their governmental officials. An agenda can be as concrete as a list of bills that are before a legislature, but also includes a series of beliefs about the existence and magnitude of problems and how they should be addressed by government, the private sector, nonprofit organizations, or through joint action by some or all of these institutions.

Agendas exist at all levels of government. Every community and every body of government—the Congress, a state legislature, a county commission—has a collection of issues that are available for discussion and disposition. All these issues can be categorized based on the extent to which an institution is prepared to make an ultimate decision to enact and implement or to reject particular policies. Furthest from enactment are issues and ideas contained in the systemic agenda, in which is contained any idea that could possibly be considered by participants in the policy process. Some ideas fail to reach this agenda because they are politically so far beyond the pale in a particular society; large-scale state ownership of the means of production, for example, is generally off the systemic agenda in the United States because it is so contrary to existing ideological commitments.

If a problem or idea is successfully elevated from the systemic agenda, it moves to the institutional agenda, a subset of the broader systemic agenda. The institutional agenda is "that list of items explicitly up for the active and serious consideration of authoritative decision makers" (Cobb and Elder 1983, 85–86). Time and resource constraints make it is impossible for institutions to handle all the problems on the systemic agenda (Hilgartner and Bosk 1988; O'Toole 1989). The limited amount of time or resources available to any institution or society means that only a limited number of issues are likely to reach the institutional agenda. Even fewer issues will reach the decision agenda, which contains items that are about to be acted upon by a governmental body. Bills, once they are introduced and heard in committee, are relatively low on the decision agenda until they are reported to the whole body for a vote. Notices of proposed rulemaking in the *Federal Register* are evidence of an issue's or problem's elevation to the decision agenda in the executive branch. Conflict may be greatest at this stage, because when a decision is reached at a particular level of government, it may trigger conflict that expands to another or higher level of government. Conflict continues and may expand.

The goal of most contending parties in the policy process is to move policies from the systemic agenda to the institutional agenda, or to prevent issues that they find inimical to their interests from reaching the institutional agenda. It is not necessary for groups to advocate policies that are linked to only one specific problem. In Kingdon's model, changes in the streams will provide opportunities for policy entrepreneurs to link their preferred solutions to problems. For example, in the case of natural disasters, a change in land-use regulations that is proposed on quality-of-life grounds may languish on the institutional agenda until a natural disaster arises, which would allow a policy entrepreneur to link land-use planning to disaster mitigation. In this way, focusing events move elements of the solution agenda closer to the decision agenda.

Just as there are many agendas at many different levels of government, the salience of issues varies with the level of government. National defense is more important at the national level, while police and education are more important at the local level. Issues also vary in their salience in different parts of the country. Earthquakes are not a salient problem in Florida, just as hurricanes are much less important in California than in the Southeast. These differences in regional salience are not a major issue in this study, as I consider federal agendas, but these differences may play a role in explaining the composition of policy communities at the national level.

THEORETICAL STRANDS IN THE STUDY OF AGENDA SETTING

While agenda setting is an important part of policy making, there is no single theory of agenda setting. Deborah Stone (1989) identifies three major strands of agenda-setting theory. The first strand examines the characteristics of the actors and institutions making policy, including the different venues in which agenda-setting and policy-making activity occur. Stone cites Kingdon's work as an example of this strand, to which I would also add Sabatier's Advocacy Coalition Framework. The second theoretical strand focuses on the nature of the problems themselves, leading to a series of principles relating to whether the problem is more likely or less likely to expand to a broader audience, thereby leading to greater attention. The nature of the actors and the nature of the problems interact with each other to promote or impede issue expansion. Theories of group mobilization and issue expansion thus explain how ideas, problems, and policies start with a rather small number of people but, for various reasons related to the nature of problems and the political skills of groups, become much more important throughout society.

The third strand explores the use of language, stories, metaphors, and symbols to advance or retard the movement of issues on the agenda. Contained in this strand is the process of social construction, by which societies collectively define and explain the nature and cause of problems. Students of the media explain how issues gain the attention of journalists, how journalists and their sources use symbols and stories to explain complex issues, and how news consumers respond to these issues and symbols. The latter two strands are important because focusing events are *used* by group leaders to mobilize support for change. The events must be socially constructed and accompanied by causal stories to influence group mobilization and issue expansion.

These three theoretical strands all contribute to understanding how focusing events gain their focal power. First, focusing events gain their power from the objective attributes of the event—the damage or injury wrought by the event, for example—but the social construction approach suggests that this power is greatly enhanced through the reduction of these events to simple, graphic, and familiar symbolic packages. Images of collapsed buildings, oiled birds, and cooling towers serve as powerful symbols of natural hazards and sometimes dangerous industrial processes that can lead to passionate reactions among recipients of these packages. The news media and advocates of policy change use these symbols and images because they are easier to package and transmit than are more complex and subtle descriptions of problems and possible solutions. Mass publics respond more readily to these symbols because they are easier to interpret than are more complex stories or analyses of public problems.

Second, theories of social construction help us to understand how problems and events are not simply objective, obvious problems that automatically gain attention simply because they are compelling issues. Rather, there are usually many different, plausible ways to conceive of issues, of which only a few dominant interpretations emerge. Indeed, the consensus construction of public problems may not be the most logical or even, ultimately, the most efficient way of thinking about a problem before searching for solutions (Gusfield 1981). The social construction of a particular problem that is highlighted by an event will have an important influence on the extent to which the issue will be expanded. This in turn will influence the policies used to deal with the problem.

Third, theories of issue expansion and group mobilization help explain *how* symbols are employed by political actors, and to what end. These theories suggest the possible strategies that defenders of the status quo employ to contain these issues. In essence, all sides of a controversy know that a focusing event is most "focal" if it expands to a broader community of interested citizens.

All these theoretical strands assume that agenda setting is not a neutral, objective, or rational process. Rather, it is the result of a society acting through political and social institutions to define the meanings of problems and the range of acceptable solutions. These strands thus describe the motivations and actions of participants in policy making and how they interact with the nature of the problems themselves. In explaining how these elements work in the politics of focusing events, I start with the more abstract ideas of symbols and social construction, and move toward the more concrete realm of mobilization and group expansion.

Agenda Setting, Symbol Propagation, and Mass Media

An important element of politics, and agenda setting particularly, is the importance of symbols and stories in the framing of public issues. These symbols and stories are framed by participants in policy making and propagated by the mass communications media.

The scholar most closely associated with the study of the symbolic dimensions of politics and policy is Murray Edelman. The influence of his pioneering books—*The Symbolic Uses of Politics* (1967) and *Constructing the Political Spectacle* (1988)—and the work of many other social scientists on the problems of symbols, interpretation, and political meaning suggest that "few political scientists today would deny that politics possesses a symbolic dimension" (Burnier 1994, 239).

Symbols condense complex ideas into easily understood, easily transmitted ideas, in which the meanings of the symbols and the underlying ideas are generally shared by the propagator of the symbol and its recipients. Debates in the United States over environmental conservation and injury have been rich with symbols and metaphors. The symbols that are most easily transmitted visually—news photographs and television images, for example—are particularly powerful, regardless of how "accurately" the underlying story is transmitted. After the Three Mile Island (TMI) nuclear power plant accident, news photographers and editorial cartoonists seized upon the hourglass-shaped cooling towers of the TMI plant (a design element shared by many nuclear plants) as an easily understood signifier of nuclear power and its dangers. The cooling tower symbol was used because it is the most prominent structural feature of most nuclear power plants, although gas- and coal-fired plants also use similarly shaped cooling towers. A more strictly accurate depiction of the dangerous part of a nuclear plant— the reactor containment structure—was not used as a symbol because it is a comparatively small part of the plant that is less prominent and recognizable. Since symbols are "shortcuts" or "stereotypes," they must be easily recognized if they are to have any power.

Similarly, a predominant symbol of the damage wreaked by the *Exxon Valdez* oil spill was the oiled sea otter. Sea otters are photogenic, gregarious, "playful" animals that are quite popular in zoos and that often elicit emotional reactions when viewed in the wild—or when seen covered in spilled oil. The image of the oiled otter played prominently in news coverage and environmental group activity, even though at least as much damage was done to fish and the Prince William Sound fishery. Fish, alas, are not as photogenic as sea otters, although fish are very important to the economy and ecosystem of Prince William Sound.

Given the power of these symbols, contending interests in a policy debate will seek to expand, downplay, or co-opt these symbols. Groups often do all three of these things simultaneously, working to promote their preferred symbols, denigrate the symbols propagated by others, and, when they cannot do so, working to appropriate the power of the symbol for their interests. The symbol of "oiled beaches," for example, leads to the symbolic *act* of "cleaning the beaches." This act was symbolic because even Exxon knew that the effort was futile, but they also knew that the effort made for good public relations and symbol creation. In this case the solution to the problem of oiled beaches may have been more harmful to the beach ecosystem than just leaving the oil alone to weather naturally (Wheelwright 1994).

This discussion of the power of symbols assumes a functionalist perspective of symbols that generally limits our understanding of symbols to who uses them, how they are used, and to what effect the symbols are used. An interpretive understanding of symbols suggests that symbols are not simply discovered, debated, and propagated, but that the symbols—and ultimately, public policies—are themselves socially constructed through language and group interaction (Burnier 1994, 241). This perspective is accommodated by most theories of the policy process. From the perspective of group political competition— from which the ideas in this book derive—a primary concern must be how groups *use* symbols in the promotion of their policy preferences. It is then assumed by contenders in policy debates that the symbols will be interpreted by most of the public in a particular way.

Modern politics and the propagation of symbols would be impossible without a mass media to communicate issues, problems, ideas, and symbols to a mass audience. Agenda-setting research in mass communications seeks to explain the propagation of information and symbols. It includes general research on agenda-setting effects (in this case meaning the relationship between news coverage and public consciousness of an issue or problem) (Rogers, Dearing, and Bergman 1992; Rogers, Dearing, and Liu 1992), and studies of the agenda-setting effect of particular events, such as ABC's television shows "The Day After" (about life after a nuclear war) and "Amerika" (about a possible Communist invasion of the United States) (Kim, Shaor-Ghaffari, and Gustainis 1990). It also studies attempts by opposing parties in disputes to influence the news media to influence the policy agenda (Smith

1991). Most research has found that the agenda-setting effect of the media is likely to be transient, subtle, and largely unpredictable. Still, most participants in political conflict believe that media coverage of dramatic events shapes mass and elite opinion. Participants in policy debate will therefore seek to shape press coverage of an event to influence substantive and symbolic information about the event that is made available to the public. News coverage of focusing events is necessary because without it there is no way for a broader public to learn of an event and perhaps mobilize in response to it. Without this mobilization, an event loses much of its focal power.

Social Construction and Agenda Setting

A social constructionist conception of agenda setting holds that agenda setting is dynamic. In this view, problems are not simply objectively big or small, benign or injurious, but instead are socially constructed through the use of symbols, beliefs, and facts to tell the story of how conditions became problems. There are many possible constructions that compete with each other to tell the story of why a problem is a problem, who is benefited or harmed by the problem, whose fault it is, and how it can be solved (Schneider and Ingram 1993; Stone 1989). The construction of a problem that fails to resonate with most citizens is unlikely to be promoted on the agenda, particularly compared to other constructions of the problem. For example, Gusfield (1981) notes that of the number of ways in which the drinking and driving problem could be addressed—as a problem of public health, control of alcohol, or even a transportation and land-use problem—the most popular construction is as a problem of individual responsibility and law enforcement. Such a construction is much more consistent with political and legal values of individuality and responsibility than are the other possible constructions.

This process of social construction leads to political actors formulating and propagating stories and symbols about social and political phenomena. One type of social construction involves what Deborah Stone calls "causal stories," in which "situations come to be seen as caused by human actions and amenable to human intervention" (Stone 1989, 281). She explains that political actors will seek to use language and appeals to value systems to seek a construction of the problem that is more amenable to their position. "Since our cultural understanding of accidents defines them as events beyond human control, causal politics is centrally concerned with moving interpretations of a situation from the realm of accident" to a realm suggesting negligent or willful human causation (Stone 1989, 284). For example, accident victims will press the claim that an accident is due to the intention of some individual or organization to cause the harm. If intentional causation cannot be proved, victims may argue that the problem is caused by "mechanical or inadvertent [negligent] causation," which removes the problem from the realm of the random act of God (Stone 1989, 281). Causal stories are important because acts of God are depicted quite differently by policy contestants than are technological accidents. Of course, the interpretation of whether a disaster is the result of an act of God or of human failing is itself the subject of debate and competition over which dominant framing will be accepted.

The social construction of an event is crucial to understanding which proposed solutions reach the agenda and with what effect. If one party can successfully argue that a problem and its harms are randomly caused, the solutions offered are less likely to reach the institutional agenda or move higher on it, since the predominant causal story is that *random* problems cannot be prevented by *rational* policy and planning. If a group successfully argues that a problem was intentionally caused by humans (willful action) or was mechanically caused (through processes under human control where harms were not willfully caused), their proposed solutions are more likely to rise on the agenda.

Policy Domains, Communities, and Policy-Making Venues

In this book, I consider two overlapping but not interchangeable concepts: policy domains and policy communities. A policy domain is the substantive subject of policy over which participants in policy making compete and compromise (see, for example, Knoke and Laumann 1982). The features of a policy domain that define its importance to participants in policy making include the relationship of the relevant policy problem to the dominant political culture, the legal environment in which policy is made (case and statute law, regulations), and the broader understanding of the nature of the problem, its causes, and the potential solutions to the problem. Also within the policy domain is the policy community, which consists of those actors, usually individuals acting on behalf of groups (Laumann and Knoke 1987), who are actively involved in policy making in a particular domain.

Most theorists of the policy process, following dominant theories of plural–elite group politics, argue that most policy is made by a core group of the most active and expert participants. If these participants make policy with little outside scrutiny or interference, in a mutually supportive relationship much like the "iron triangle" model of subsystem government, the community can be said to be a policy monopoly (Baumgartner and Jones 1993). Many communities in public policy are not, however, policy monopolies: environmental policy, for example, tends to be rather open and quite contentious. These communities generally form into one to four advocacy coalitions. Defining the policy community in terms of one or more advocacy coalitions prevents us from assuming, as in the iron triangle model of policy subsystems, that policy making is tightly integrated and closed to entry. On the other hand, the advocacy coalition framework suggests that policy is made through the patterned interaction of individual actors who are well-known to each other and who represent a range of groups and interests, including government, the private sector, the media, and academia.

A key element of the theory of focusing events is an assumption that the boundaries of the policy community ebb and flow with the course of events. I thus define *policy community* more broadly than other students of the policy process because the changes in the boundaries of the community that are wrought by an event are very important to postevent politics. Policy making is most often led by the most active and knowledgeable participants, who form advocacy coalitions, with sometimes less informed and more episodic participation by actors whose entry into the policy community is triggered by a focusing event. Indeed, as I show in later chapters, the entry and exit of new participants in the community, or the invigoration of persistent but marginal actors, is an important outcome of focusing events.

The policy community concept is very important to this study because policy communities sometimes coalesce without forming advocacy coalitions. In the hurricane policy case in chapter 3, there is no true advocacy coalition, but rather a fairly loose policy community at the federal level that has failed to coalesce. It is more profitable to consider this a policy community rather than a coalition of any sort. Second, an important part of the theory of focusing events is the assumption that most policy communities—but not advocacy coalitions—are fluid and permeable. Many actors enter and exit a policy community when something triggers their participation, whether they are or are not normally active in it. The earthquake and hurricane policy communities, in particular, tend to have highly changeable membership, depending on whether an event is on the agenda. Focusing events, in short, affect the agenda of a policy community, the composition of that community, and the substance of the items on the agenda in that community.

Mobilization and Group Expansion

Social constructionist understandings of agenda setting complement E.E. Schattschneider's theories of group mobilization and participation, which rest on his oft-cited contention that issues are more likely to be elevated to agenda status if the scope of conflict is broadened. There are two key ways in which traditionally disadvantaged (losing) groups expand the scope of conflict. First, groups "go public" with a problem by using symbols and images to induce greater media and public sympathy for their cause. Environmental groups dramatize their causes by pointing to symbols and images of allegedly willful or negligent humanly caused environmental damage (for example, the *Exxon Valdez* spill). Second, groups that lose in the first stage of a political conflict can appeal to a "higher," more authoritative, national decision-making level. This explains the trend toward nationalization of American politics, as losing parties continually appeal to state and then federal institutions for a hearing or for redress, hoping that in the process they will attract other partisans to their cause. Conversely, it shows how dominant groups work to contain conflict to ensure that it does not spread and grow out of control. The debates over nationalization and coordination of oil spill and disaster relief policies are natural outgrowths of these tendencies. The underlying theory of these tendencies dates to Madison's defense, in Federalist 10, of the constitutional system as a mechanism to contain political conflict.

Schattschneider's theories of issue expansion help to explain how in-groups retain control over problem definition and the way such problems are suppressed by dominant actors in policy making. These actors form policy monopolies, which attempt to keep problems and underlying policy issues low on the agenda. Policy communities, defined by their substantive and symbolic commitments (Burstein 1991), use agreed-upon symbols to construct their visions of problems, causation, and solution. As long as these images and symbols are maintained throughout society, or remain largely invisible and unquestioned, agenda access for groups that do not share these images is likely to be difficult; change is less likely until the out-group's construction of the problem becomes more prevalent. If alternative selection is the sine qua non of power, an important corollary is that powerful groups retain power by working to keep the public and out-groups unaware of underlying problems, alternative constructions of problems, or alternatives to their resolution (Gaventa 1980).

There are times when control over agenda access cannot be maintained. Baumgartner and Jones (1993) argue that loss of agenda control leads to greater access to policy making for out-groups and greater attention to problems. This, in turn, tends to increase negative public attitudes toward the status quo. In the long run, this process can produce lasting institutional agenda changes that break up preexisting policy monopolies. When the keepers of the policy monopoly find it impossible to contain agenda access or expansion, out-groups are likely to become involved. In domains dominated by a policy monopoly the involvement of previously excluded groups is often a necessary, but not sufficient, precursor to policy change.

Change is not always resisted, however, by political elites. Cobb and Elder (1983) argue that, when political elites seek change, they try to mobilize publics to generate mass support for an issue, which supports elite efforts to move issues further up the agenda. I argue that such efforts can constitute either attempts to broaden the ambit of existing policy monopolies or attempts by some political elites (such as the president and his staff) to circumvent the policy monopoly established by interest groups, the bureaucracy, and subcommittees (the classic iron triangle model). The president or other key political actors may be able to further enhance the focusing power of an event by visiting a disaster or accident scene, thereby affording the event even greater symbolic weight. The use of focusing events by members of the "establishment" to examine problems and pursue solutions is exemplified by the earthquake policy community described in chapter 3.

THE SPECIAL ROLE OF POLICY ENTREPRENEURS

A particular kind of actor who is involved in agenda setting is the policy entrepreneur, whose role is discussed throughout this study. Policy entrepreneurs are participants who are constantly involved in the policy community because of their technical expertise in their field, because of their political expertise and ability to broker deals that lead to new programs and policies, and because of their connection to the problem as representatives of a particular constituency. Policy entrepreneurs are particularly important because they lead groups and coalitions that seek to use focusing events for their symbolic potential, thereby advancing issues on the agenda.

Policy entrepreneurs become involved in politics for a number of reasons: they represent an interest group, they represent a constituency (such as legislators), they want to promote their values or beliefs, or they simply enjoy the intellectual stimulation and competition of the political process (Kingdon 1995). Policy entrepreneurs press for policy change that favors their interests during normal, non-event-driven politics, but may find themselves in different roles after events, with some policy entrepreneurs calling for fairly comprehensive policy change while others argue that change, if necessary at all, should be more measured.

LOOKING AHEAD

In the next chapter, I turn to a framework for the study of focusing events. The framework includes a definition of potential focusing events and shows how that definition can guide the selection of domains in which focusing events can be studied. From this definition, I suggest that certain features of potential focusing events can make them more focal, and the absence of them can make the events less focal. These features guide the collection of the data used to assess event influence on the media and institutional agendas.

In chapter 3 I examine the politics of policy making in the wake of earthquakes and hurricanes. At first earthquakes and hurricanes might seem to be subject to similar focusing event politics. Yet I find that the policy communities that address these events are quite different. I find that the earthquake community is much better defined and contains more active professionals who deal with earthquake issues for a living and who are available to testify before Congress in the wake of an earthquake. By contrast, the hurricane domain does not contain a readily identifiable cadre of policy entrepreneurs and professionals ready to explain what happened and what needs to be done in the wake of a hurricane. I explain this phenomenon by examining the institutional and political environment in which policy making on earthquakes and hurricanes takes place.

In chapter 4 I examine the influence of oil spills on the institutional agenda. Oil spills are different from natural disasters because their direct harms to human populations are not as clear as are harms from natural disasters. However, oil spills do engage active environmental groups. This results in greater group conflict and the availability of a number of active, vocal groups to exploit the symbolic and political power of these events. As I show in chapter 4, the symbols involved in oil spills are quite rich and lend themselves to use by environmental groups to press for policy change.

Chapter 5 analyzes nuclear power plant accidents as focusing events. Nuclear power is of course a very contentious issue, and its future continues to be debated in the United States. The extent and gravity of nuclear power plant accidents is hard to gauge, since there have been so few major accidents that gained widespread attention. Only one such event—the Three Mile Island accident in 1979—

approached the level of attention received by the *Exxon Valdez* oil spill, Hurricane Camille, or the Loma Prieta earthquake. The nuclear power community, at least before the Three Mile Island accident, was dominated by scientific and technical experts who were dealing with very new technology and very little accumulated experience in nuclear power generation. Their debates over nuclear safety were much more concerned with the probability of disaster than were debates in the other communities. This case provides a better understanding this type of technical, often conjectural, policy making.

The study concludes in chapter 6 with a discussion of how focusing events can lead to policy change by promoting learning about policy failure. I also consider two types of focusing events beyond those studied here: highly unusual events that have only occurred once or twice, and thereby provide few opportunities for comparison with similar events, and rather ordinary events that are focal because of an extraordinary feature of the event.

2

A Theory of Focusing Events and Agenda Change

Efforts to create and improve theories of the policy process have met with significant challenges since policy studies emerged as a distinctive branch of the social sciences in the 1960s. One of these challenges comes in clearly defining key concepts. As discussed in the previous chapter, many students of the policy process have described focusing events by using different terminology and overlapping but inconsistent definitions. Beyond the problem of multiple implicit definitions of the phenomenon, there appears to be no single definition of a focusing event that can be applied prospectively to what I term *potential* focusing events. Such a definition is important because it allows us to define potential focusing events without resorting to ad hoc or post hoc characterizations of these events. I thus begin this chapter by providing a more precise definition of what I call *potential focusing events*. This definition is important because the theory rests on the assumption that the focal nature of focusing events is variable along a range of possible attributes. This definition is particularly useful in selecting areas of policy making, known as policy domains, in which to isolate sets of potential focusing events for more systematic analysis.

A second challenge in the study of public policy lies in clearly specifying and explaining important forces that lead to policy-making outcomes. This is particularly true in the passing mentions of focusing events in policy studies, where the attributes of events that make them focal are rarely if ever specified within a more comprehensive theory of the policy process. I propose to close this gap by outlining a framework for understanding the focal power of events. This framework was designed to be subject to empirical testing, as outlined in greater detail here and as demonstrated in the case studies in chapters 3, 4, and 5.

DEFINING POTENTIAL FOCUSING EVENTS

Kingdon's and Cobb and Elder's definitions of focusing events rely heavily on post hoc characterizations of the importance of particular events in agenda change. Their definitions do not go beyond these events to suggest what it is about a particular event that makes it *focal*. However, their references to these events suggest that the "focal power" of events is continuous, with some events being more focal than others. For example, some focusing events may be focal because they affect many people in some way, such as in a natural disaster that affects a broad geographic area. Other events may be focal because they reveal the possibility of greater potential disaster, as in a nuclear power plant accident. Another event may be focal because it motivated a number of interest groups and policy entrepreneurs to take action to deal with the issues exemplified by the event. However, simply having these attributes does not mean that an event will automatically gain attention or, in my terms, be focal. Any such event is therefore a *potential* focusing event. The first step in an analysis of these events is to define focusing events in such a way that we can identify a policy domain in which such events are likely to be important, rather than simply retrospectively choosing such events across multiple, sometimes dissimilar, domains. Choosing events to study in this manner would encourage researchers to rely on description rather than on more rigorous empirical analysis.

A theory based on such a definition need not predict whether and how a particular event that occurs at any particular moment might be focal. Instead, the definition should define the things that make events potentially focal, which in turn will suggest the types of domains in which focusing events might occur. The definition should also provide important clues as to the nature of postevent politics. This helps us to avoid simply choosing a series of candidate events from a number of different policy domains. Such a definition would therefore cause us to look to domains in which events occur, rather than the events themselves. With this in mind, a definition of *potential* focusing events must not rely on post hoc categorizations of individual, disparate events.

I define a *potential focusing event* as *an event that is sudden, relatively rare, can be reasonably defined as harmful or revealing the possibility of potentially greater future harms, inflicts harms or suggests potential harms that are or could be concentrated on a definable geographical area or community of interest, and that is known to policy makers and the public virtually simultaneously.* These features of focusing events are matters of degree; particular types of events are more or less rare, are more or less concentrated in a particular population, and are more or less harmful to the community or a subset of it. A result of such an event might be a finding by interest groups, government leaders, policy entrepreneurs, the news media, or members of the public of new problems, new attention to existing but dormant (in terms of their standing on the agenda) problems, and, potentially, a search for solutions in the wake of perceived policy failure. The magnitude of the influence of an event on communities, and thus the extent to which an event is focal, is variable; the focal importance of an event is therefore continuous (more or less focal), not dichotomous (is or is not focal).

The first criterion of potential focusing events is that such events happen suddenly, with little or no warning. Problems that slowly gain or lose public interest as a result of gradual accretion of indicators of a problem and the deployment of conflicting facts and stories will more gradually wax and wane on the agenda. Their movement up or down the agenda may be promoted or resisted by constant group competition. Sudden events, on the other hand, are associated with "spikes" of intense interest and agenda activity that are attributable to a particular event. Interest groups that seek to prevent these issues from becoming elevated on the agenda will find it very difficult to keep them off the news agenda and institutional agendas. Conversely, groups that seek to elevate an issue on the agenda can use these events to attract greater attention to the problem revealed by the event.

Second, a potential focusing event is generally rare, and, as a consequence, is unpredictable and unplanned. Compare, for example, airplane crashes to automobile accidents. The focal power of individual automobile accidents is rather low, because they happen daily, usually affect a few people, and because as a society we have learned how to weigh the daily deaths of dozens of people against the benefits of greater personal mobility. Each automobile accident taken by itself thus has relatively little focal power; rather, it is the aggregation of these accidents that can lead to greater attention to the problem of highway safety. The automobile safety campaigns of the 1960s were motivated by the alarming growth in the aggregate numbers of highway injuries and deaths, not by individual accidents. Automobile manufacturers joined this debate by arguing that the studies were flawed or that drivers were the cause of fatal accidents, not defects in automobile design. The lack of a single, dramatic event made this a debate about statistics and plausible causal theories, but not about individual events.

By contrast with numerous events scattered across space and time, such as thousands of separate automobile crashes nationwide, potential focusing events gain a great deal of their agenda-setting and mobilizing power by aggregating harms. Compared to indicators of problems in health or medicine, for example, which are slow to develop and to be perceived by analysts, "in transportation, something that goes wrong is often already preaggregated. An airplane goes down, killing hundreds of people at once rather than killing one patient at a time" (Kingdon 1995, 96).

Airplane crashes are potentially focal because they are unexpected. We can assume that an airplane will crash somewhere at some time in the future, but the wreck of a *particular* flight at a *particular* place and time is usually unexpected. Such an accident is unexpected *because* it is rare; we generally do not expect an airplane to crash on any given day, but do expect a certain number of daily fatal car wrecks. The death of 150 people in one airline crash is therefore far more news-worthy—and worthy of policy makers' attention—than 150 fatal one-person automobile accidents. This is because of the aggregation of fatalities, the publication of passenger lists that attach names and home-towns to crash victims (Perrow 1984, 127), and the drama of the crash and the ensuing investigations. These elements of plane crashes are eagerly covered by the news media. This focal power is reflected in accident investigations: the now-familiar search for and analysis of the "black box" data recorder; the efforts by the National Transportation Safety Board (NTSB), the FAA, the airline, and the aircraft maker to fix a cause; the public hearings; and, usually, the NTSB's findings of the cause of the accident. Clearly, no such highly visible effort is ex-pended on 150 separate automobile accidents.[1]

A rare event is also one that is generally unpredictable with a reasonable degree of certainty. One cannot generally predict or forecast the number of airline crashes that will happen in a given day, week, or even year, because they have become so rare that we have been unable to establish any sort of trends or patterns of airplane accidents. Automobile accidents happen often, on the other hand, and we can generally predict, with some accuracy, that a certain number of acci-dents will occur in a given period and that some fraction of them will be fatal. Of course, the trend can change from year to year, and fatalities per mile traveled have declined due to improvements in automobile design and performance. But these improvements are detectable within the broader trend of the aggregate data, not at a particular point. Earthquakes, an important case in this study, are remarkably difficult to predict, in large part because we do not have sufficient data over a long period of time to even know whether there are cycles of greater or lesser earthquake activity. Even if we did know it was coming, we may never be able to fix the *precise* location or time of the next big earthquake. The inability to predict such events tends to increase soci-ety's fear of such disasters; the less predictable a disaster, the more "dreadful" the event, and therefore the more frightening the possibility of such an event. The rarity of an event is closely related to its sudden-ness; rare events cannot be predicted, and thus strike with little or no warning. More frightening events are more focal because they increase attention on events about which society as a whole would likely wish to know more, so that their effects can be mitigated.

Third, a potential focusing event affects a large number of people. These people can be in the same geographic area, as in the case of natural disasters and most industrial accidents (the domains considered in this study), or in communities of interest. Communities of interest are composed of people and groups who share an interest in a particular policy issue. For example, fishers nationwide were interested in the *Exxon Valdez* spill, oil spill policy generally, and any policy outcomes from the spill. These communities can be geographically diffuse, and therefore more difficult to precisely define. The harms revealed by a potential focusing event can be current, actual harms, potentially greater future harms that are highlighted by the event (the contrast between a "merely" damaging earthquake and the much feared "Big One," for example), or both. When current harms are sufficiently large, they are likely to be the center of attention. In domains where the consequences of a larger event than the current event on the agenda could be catastrophic, the revelation of potential harms is quite important. In nuclear power, for example, there has not yet been a disastrous domestic nuclear power accident, but large-scale accidents that came close to disaster, such as the 1979 Three Mile Island accident, can be quite focal because they foreshadow the possibility of an even more serious accident.

Finally, the public and the most informed members of the policy community learn of a potential focusing event virtually simultaneously. These events can very rapidly alter mass and elite consciousness of a social problem. I say "virtually" because the most active members of a policy community may learn of an event some hours before the general public. For example, the *Exxon Valdez* ran aground just after midnight in Alaska, or just after 4:00 A.M. on the East Coast. Most people were asleep when the spill occurred, but learned of it through the morning radio or TV news, or late morning newspapers. Certain members of the policy community, however, such as key employees of the Exxon Corporation, the local Coast Guard contingent, fishers in south-central Alaska, and others with a direct interest in the event, learned of the spill within minutes or hours. Still, the span of time that passed between local and national knowledge—or between elite and mass knowledge—of the spill was far too short for any particular interest to effectively contain news of the spill and, therefore, contain the influence of the event on the agenda.

Since the event comes to mass and elite consciousness simultaneously, issue containment or expansion strategies must be employed hurriedly and almost on the fly; neither side of the ensuing debate is able to time the occurrence of events and plan, in any detail, their responses to them. In short, potential focusing events are important because they are so hard to keep off the agenda and, by definition, will become more difficult to contain as they gain broader attention.

Of all these elements of the definition of potential focusing event, the feature that distinguishes this process—and focusing events generally—from more "routine" politics is that potential focusing events often happen quite suddenly, and therefore are fixed to a particular time, both in media coverage of the event and in any subsequent policy-making activities. Because of their suddenness, problems revealed by potential focusing events are different from problems that are identified over a longer period. Because potential focusing events are fixed to a particular time, participants in policy making can more readily cite a focusing event as a proximate cause of agenda change or the need for subsequent policy change. Most people inside and outside the policy-making process will share some understanding of the broader meaning of the event when just its name is invoked. When one says "the Loma Prieta earthquake" or "the *Exxon Valdez* oil spill," little more needs to be said to explain what the event was about and why it was important.

Because potential focusing events are fixed in time, they can attract attention from a range of actors virtually simultaneously. The strategic advantages to be gained from planning to introduce new initiatives, or using a contrived event, such as a well-publicized protest rally, to highlight long-standing issues, are unavailable when the event is unanticipated by all potential participants in policy making. By contrast with ordinary politics, focusing events cause all participants to start their efforts to expand or contain an issue at virtually the same time.

Since a potential focusing event levels the field in this way, it creates advantages for traditionally less powerful groups that seek to advance proposed policy changes. In contrast to "routine" or "normal" politics, potential focusing events lead to near-immediate attention to the problem, giving change-oriented groups and leaders an opportunity to mobilize by pointing to the event as an exemplar of what is wrong with existing policy. This attention provides opportunities for group mobilization and issue expansion, both of which are usually anathema to members of a status quo oriented advocacy coalition or policy monopoly, depending on which most accurately describes the particular policy domain. As Baumgartner and Jones (1993) found, greater attention to a problem is often a precursor to policy change. Potential focusing events generate this attention and increase opportunities for expansion and mobilization of group membership.

While these characteristics are shared by potential focusing events, each event is unique. The process and ease of defining the problem as important varies with the unique characteristics of the event and the unique characteristics of the political environment in which the event occurred. This definition of potential focusing events does not fully describe all the important elements of each event; it aids, first, in isolating the domains in which such events are more likely to be important and, second, in identifying shared features of these events that lead to greater attention to the problem. For example, Kingdon (1995, 99) argues that focusing events need to be accompanied by evidence of whether the revealed problem is particularly important or relatively unimportant. This process of defining the relationship between the event and the problems revealed by the event defines a great deal of the similarities and differences between policy domains, as revealed in the following chapters.

CANDIDATE EVENTS AND CANDIDATE DOMAINS

When considering the definition of focusing events and the features of the politics that surround them, it is worthwhile to identify representative events that may serve as potential focusing events and that suggest candidate domains for study. This does not mean that we should select disparate events. Rather, a review of recent, highly visible events can reveal the kinds of domains that contain numerous events that fit the definition of potential focusing events. These events captured the attention of many people and, as will be explored in later chapters, served as examples of danger, damage, and destruction.

- The 1971 San Fernando Earthquake occurred, fortunately, in the early morning hours. Had the earthquake struck during rush hour, many more commuters would have been killed or injured by collapsing highway overpasses. Damage to hospitals, most notably a Veterans Administration Hospital, highlighted the vulnerability of these vital facilities to earthquakes. Federal law passed soon after the earthquake provided aid to private hospitals damaged by the San Fernando earthquake and other natural disasters, while the State of California began a program to reinforce highway overpasses against the shaking of future earthquakes (Gates 1972). The San Fernando earthquake also began a process that culminated in the National Earthquake Hazards Reduction Act of 1977.
- In 1969, Hurricane Camille struck the Gulf Coast, with the brunt of the storm striking New Orleans and coastal Louisiana and Mississippi. Widespread coastal flooding ensued and 256 people were killed. Similarly, in 1989 Hurricane Hugo struck historic Charleston, South Carolina, and its environs. Expensive beach homes on barrier islands were destroyed but, soon after the storm, plans were made for rebuilding damaged properties. This led federal, state, and local officials to reexamine policies that failed to discourage building in areas most subject to the hurricane hazard.

- The 1989 *Exxon Valdez* oil spill was the largest-ever spill from a tanker in American coastal waters. Over 11 million gallons of crude oil were spilled. The damage to the fishing and tourism industries was incalculable, and considerable controversy still rages over the exact extent of damage and who is at fault. In the wake of this spill, Congress passed the Oil Pollution Act of 1990, overcoming more than fourteen years of deadlock over revisions to federal oil spill policy (Davidson 1990; Keeble 1991; Randle 1991; Wheelwright 1994).
- In 1979 the Three Mile Island Unit 2 nuclear power plant, near Harrisburg, Pennsylvania, suffered the most serious commercial nuclear power plant accident in American history. The event was the product of an almost unimaginable conjunction of human errors and mechanical failures. Plans were readied to evacuate the surrounding area, the governor recommended that children and pregnant women within ten miles evacuate, and the nation anxiously awaited word that the possible meltdown of the reactor core had been averted. The ensuing damage to the reactor was so great that the reactor will never be repaired and reused. The damage to the nuclear power industry was also great. The accident reinforced growing skepticism about the safety and costs of nuclear power generation, and provided the recently created Nuclear Regulatory Commission the first opportunity to flex its regulatory muscle (Baumgartner and Jones 1993; Perrow 1984).

While different in the details, these events share important characteristics. These events all meet at least most of the criteria outlined in the definition: they are rare, harmful, unpredictable events that we know from the historical record left considerable discussion and controversy in their wake. They occurred quite suddenly, with lead times ranging from almost zero (oil spills, earthquakes, nuclear power plants) to days (hurricanes). Although it is known that such events will probably happen sometime, it is usually unknown when or where they will occur next. These events caused substantial property and environmental damage or raised the specter of environmental catastrophe. The natural disasters killed hundreds of people and injured many more. Because of their suddenness and the drama of death and damage, these events attracted a great deal of news media attention. The dramatic pictures and stories that accompany these events are particularly compelling subjects for coverage by the news media. The extent to which this immediate attention to near-term costs of a disaster translates into more systematic and comprehensive responses to the underlying problems revealed by focusing events is an important issue that is addressed in this book.

Most importantly, these events suggest that there are other events in these domains that may also be focal. In recent decades there have been several earthquakes, hurricanes, oil spills, and (rather minor) nuclear power plant accidents in the United States. For the most part the harms associated with these events are measurable by using fairly standard measures of damage: fatalities, property damage, or oil spilled, for example. In oil spills and, in particular, the nuclear power accidents, the measures of damage are less clear and potentially more controversial than the measures of harm in the natural disasters. The choice of these particular domains allows us to understand the differences between natural disasters, which are usually considered "natural" or "acts of God," and industrial accidents, which are often portrayed as humanly caused "accidents" that come about either through the inevitable failures of human systems or as the outcome of more troublesome human neglect.

There is a considerable difference between pointing out these *domains* as containing potential focusing events and simply selecting *events* that we know have been focal or important or "big." Having advanced these domains as candidates for study of focusing events, we can select *all* such events over several years to understand which of these events are or are not focal. This is the method employed in this book. The events we suspect will be most focal usually are the most focal. However, by looking at *all* damaging earthquakes, hurricanes, oil spills, and nuclear accidents in a particular period, we can compare more focal events with less focal events within particular domains.

A FRAMEWORK FOR THE STUDY OF FOCUSING EVENTS

In this section I provide a framework for studying focusing event politics. This framework directly informs the collection and analysis of quantitative data presented in the following chapters. But the definition is not simply intended to provide a series of variables for quantitative analysis. The definition and the framework also aid in understanding the institutional and individual reactions to these events that are further described in the case studies.

For conceptual clarity and greater analytic simplicity, I conceive of focusing event politics as proceeding in two phases. In the first phase after the event, the news media immediately respond to event attributes that are most closely related to the event itself: the level of damage, for example, or the number of people effected. The second phase involves a longer-term reaction by those active in policy making to political factors associated with the event. In this phase, the rarity and the scope of the event are key variables, as are the amount of news coverage (which sometimes impels government to act upon a problem), the extent to which important elite and group attitudes after the event influence attention to the problem, and the extent to which group mobilization influences attention to the problem.

As discussed in greater detail later in the study, the greater amount of activity in these two phases usually occurs during a two-year post-event period. This two-phase construction is empirically and logically sensible for two reasons. First, the data I review in the case studies show that the most intensive press coverage of a disaster or accident comes within weeks of an event, while the peak institutional response to the event comes between three amd six months after the event. Second, this is sensible because clearly the news media, because of news-gathering norms and imperatives, concentrate on immediate, sudden events and devote considerable attention to them for a very short time before turning to the next important news event (Bennett 1995). Institutions such as the Congress, on the other hand, are constrained by their rules, procedures, and folkways, and often cannot react as rapidly as the news media. Indeed, it is often news media coverage in the immediate aftermath of an event that impels Congress to take up the issue. But Congress will often take longer to investigate an issue, as more information becomes available to members and committees.

The News Media: Immediate Reaction to Focusing Events

The initial reaction to a focusing event is detectable in the news media. News imperatives make sudden, novel, and injurious events particularly attractive for news coverage. Environmental catastrophes and natural disasters often provide much more photogenic stories than do problems that rely on changes in indicators for their purported urgency. Students of the media have long known that news outlets are often the first on the scene with descriptions, some more lurid than accurate, of important events. The news media are a particularly important element of this study because greater levels of news coverage are closely associated with greater levels of institutional attention to public problems (Smith 1992). But the media's influence goes beyond its ability to pressure policy makers to pay attention to problems.

The news media affect a broader population than just those most directly involved with shaping the institutional agenda. Theories of issue expansion (Schattschneider 1960/1975), democratization of agenda access (Cobb and Elder 1983), and erosion of policy monopolies (Baumgartner and Jones 1993) cite the opening of policy domains to greater public scrutiny as an important precursor to agenda change (and, eventually, policy change). One way that domains are opened to scrutiny is through the activities of the news media. Some domains are pried open because of scandal (Kemp 1984) or the activities of disgruntled members of the policy community, who leak information to the press and to interest groups who seek to elevate issues on the agenda. In other instances groups will "arouse" or "provoke" the news media to devote greater scrutiny to an issue or a problem (Cobb and Elder 1983, 142–143).

There is often little need for groups to provoke the press into immediate coverage of a major dramatic event. The drama and novelty of a potential focusing event is often sufficient to elevate the issue on the media agenda. This is an important difference between potential focusing events and "media events" that are largely preplanned by contenders in a political controversy. Over the long term, groups that want policy change must exploit a potential focusing event to keep the issue fresh and relatively high on the agenda, lest the problem recede from the media and institutional agendas. But in the immediate term— three to six months after the event—news coverage of the problem revealed by the event will be easily discernible and at a significantly greater level than before the event.

There are three elements of focusing events that are most likely to induce media coverage of a focusing event and that can be readily modeled. The first of these elements is the scope of the event; that is, the number of people somehow affected by the event. In a natural disaster, for example, the number of people in the declared disaster area represents the scope of the disaster. Scope is important to news coverage because drama, an important part of the framing of a news story, is usually depicted in human terms (Bennett 1995), such as how many people are hurt and how much damage was done. The more people who are affected by an event, the more dramatic the event, and therefore the more focal the event. A disaster is only a disaster if it affects human populations in some way. Many large (Richter magnitude 7.0 or greater) earthquakes have struck in the Aleutian islands, but they tend to have far less focal power than "smaller" but very damaging earthquakes that strike populated areas of southern California.

Events that strike populated areas also strike where there is a greater concentration of news media personnel. National news tends to originate from the few large cities in which television networks and national newspapers, such as the *New York Times*, have bureaus (Epstein 1973). An event in California, where more people are affected and where more journalists are available to report it, is likely to get more attention than an event in a less-populated area with few people either affected by the event or available to report it. An extreme example of this effect is the 1989 Loma Prieta earthquake, which not only struck a populated area, but also struck as game three of the 1989 World Series was to start. That the series was being played between both Bay Area baseball franchises ensured a rather greater news media presence in the area than was normal, even for this large metropolitan area.

Second, potential focusing events are those in which harms done by a disaster or accident are visible and highly tangible. These events are likely to gain greater media attention than are events in which evidence of harms cannot be photographed or tangibly described. In the case of natural disasters, visible and tangible harms include deaths and property damage. In the case of oil spills, volume of spilled oil is the most obvious harm. This manifestation of harm need not be the most injurious aspect of the event, but need only be the harm that gets the greatest attention. For example, as I show in chapter 4, the volume of oil spilled is the best predictor of news coverage of oil spills, even though the sheer volume of oil spilled is not necessarily the best indicator of the harm done by the spill. Spilled oil is the most *visible* sign of harm, however, and is therefore an important determinant of news attention. These manifestations of harm give journalists a set of powerful symbols with which to depict the problems revealed by an event. The result is that, from an agenda-setting perspective, the most visible harms are the most important harms.

Third, the rarity or novelty of the event is important because run-of-the-mill events are unlikely to gain focal power because of their commonness. For example, small earthquakes that rattle dishes, or small oil spills of a few thousand gallons, are weekly or monthly events that will gain very little attention. But rare events are also the most dramatic. Rarity is most often a function of the size of an event; events are often calibrated against prior events, such as when an event is cited as "the largest oil spill since the *Exxon Valdez*" or "the biggest earthquake since Loma Prieta." But size is not the only consideration. The second of two large accidents or disasters within a short period will not have the same focal impact as a second event several years after the first one, because the second event is no longer rare, and the drama and symbolism of the first event are hard to recreate so soon.

Political Reactions to Events and Their Influence on the Institutional Agenda

While the news media tend to react immediately to events and then move on to other, "hotter" stories as the novelty of the event subsides, the event signals the beginning of a longer-term process of institutional response; groups and policy entrepreneurs vie over the interpretation of the event and its substantive implications for greater attention and ultimate policy change. Several elements of the postevent environment should be readily detectable and will lead to greater institutional attention to a problem.

The first element is the news coverage of an event.[2] News media coverage is an extremely important influence on group mobilization and, ultimately, on institutional agenda activity. "For an item or an issue to acquire public recognition, its supporters must have either access to the mass media or the resources necessary to reach people" (Cobb and Elder 1983, 86). Baumgartner and Jones "find that media coverage does indeed correspond to official concerns" (1993, 49), while Smith (1992, 9) notes that policy makers' most important sources of information after sudden events are the *New York Times* and the *Washington Post*. Focusing events provide prochange groups with a significant strategic advantage: they relieve activists of the task of persuading or cajoling the media to devote space or time to covering their pet issues. Rather, potential focusing events can be so large and dramatic that they gain news coverage virtually automatically.

The second critical postevent political activity is the mobilization of prochange forces in direct response to the event. This mobilization may be followed by some countermobilization by groups that support the existing status quo; these groups tend to form or maintain an advocacy coalition in defense of the existing policy monopoly. Mobilization is clearly a goal of prochange groups that seek to broaden the scope of conflict to involve other actors whom they hope will be sympathetic to their position. Baumgartner and Jones showed that greater attention to a problem—in other words, broadening the scope of conflict—usually led to more negative assessments of current policy, and consequently to pressures on the policy monopoly to open up policy making and accept change.

Focusing events are particularly important to individuals or groups that are part of relatively weak advocacy coalitions. Groups that have traditionally struggled to gain a hearing or see their preferences translated into policy (such as fishing interests in Alaska in their debates with the oil industry or antinuclear power groups before Three Mile Island) can use focusing events to gain agenda access in at least two ways. Groups can point to the event itself as a powerful symbol and accurate description of the underlying problem. An oil spill, for example, provides powerful symbols of the risks of petroleum extraction and shipment; these symbols are less important in periods of "normal" politics (i.e., politics that do not follow or reference a particular event) and fade in importance as the most recent event fades into the past. Beyond out-groups' efforts to exploit symbols derived from the event, a major event occupies a certain amount of agenda space that can neither be ignored by the attentive public nor be contained by established members of the policy community. In the initial phase of an event, the symbols of the event are presented to mass publics and opinion leaders through the communications media in relatively raw and undifferentiated form, but these images are followed by prochange forces' repetition of the most important and vivid images and symbols. For example, a predominant image of the *Exxon Valdez* oil spill was oiled wildlife, especially sea otters. This image was then repeatedly used by environmental groups as a way to drive home the need for stricter oil spill legislation.

If this is assumption is true, it should be possible to find greater group activity after focusing events. A primary indicator of group activity in national policy making is testimony from group leaders before congressional committees. Congressional testimony is the most common lobbying technique employed by interest groups (Davidson and Oleszek 1994, 298). This is entirely sensible. The main task of groups competing in the American political system is not access to elected officials per se as much as it is access to the institutional agenda, which is controlled by elected and high-level appointed officials. This study uses committee hearings as a major indicator of the institutional agenda, particularly because they are such a popular venue for group competition in policy making and because legislative proceedings are more open and are better and more consistently documented than the executive branch's.

Baumgartner and Jones argue that the breakdown of a policy monopoly is, by definition, a result of other voices being heard in a domain. I tie this increase in new voices to particular events and propose that focusing events can result in greater activity by prochange groups than by pro-status-quo groups. If the event leads to a large mobilization of prochange groups compared to antichange groups, it is focal, and institutional agenda change is the result. If the focusing event shifts the preferences of the policy community away from maintaining the status quo, the first evidence of this shift will be the increased inclusion of groups that had previously been underrepresented or unrepresented in the policy community. Such groups are more likely to exploit an event to advance their policy preferences. For example, after the *Exxon Valdez* oil spill in 1989, fishing groups were far more visible in congressional hearings on oil spill policy than before the spill. Investigating this proposition requires that we examine group public relations activity. A primary indicator of such activity is the volume and tone of testimony delivered to congressional committees.

In-groups are also made active by focusing events. However, if an event threatens to reduce the power of in-groups and threatens their control over the agenda, establishment groups will respond defensively to focusing events, downplaying their significance and providing officials and the public with alternative causal stories. Such groups are much more likely to argue that the event is not as important as claimed by opposing groups, that existing policy is able to deal with the problem, or that, if new policy is needed, the policy proposed by the contending groups would be ineffective or counterproductive.

A second key variable is event *scope*. The scope of an event's effects is important to institutional agenda setting for a simple reason: the more people (constituents) are affected by an event, the more likely there will be a number of elected officials available to press an issue upward on the agenda. An earthquake in the Los Angeles metropolitan area, for example, will likely induce action of some sort from several members of Congress, while an earthquake in Alaska can only directly mobilize one representative and two senators. Members will be mobilized by constituent requests for help in expediting disaster relief, but are also likely to anticipate needs and elevate the issue before constituents are mobilized. In either case, events that affect many people will be more important than those that affect few.

The "tone" variable is an assessment of the attitudes of witnesses at congressional hearings toward existing policy. It can be supportive of current policy or critical of it. Changes in tone also provide some evidence of the introduction of new ideas or attitudes toward policy change in a policy community. "Tone also provides a clue to the critical points in an issue's development. When the tone is changing rapidly, systems are likely to undergo change. When attention increases following a change in tone, rapid change is almost certain" (Baumgartner and Jones 1993, 51). Baumgartner and Jones tracked the decay of policy monopolies and cited changes in tone as an early and important element in policy monopoly breakdown. I suggest, in a different way than Baumgartner and Jones, that the attention to focusing events and overall policy attitude change *simultaneously* in the wake of an event. Thus, when the attitude toward current policy as expressed by groups is most negative, institutional agenda change is likely to result as this negative attitude toward policy triggers efforts to develop improved policies. This influence is enhanced by the vivid imagery that keeps focusing events closer to the top of the agenda, at least for a while.

POLICY DOMAIN CHARACTERISTICS AND THEIR INFLUENCE ON AGENDA SETTING

There are important differences between policy domains that influence agenda change. These differences result from the interaction of event attributes with domain characteristics. These differences can be summarized in three categories: the extent of policy community *organization*, the extent of public *participation* in a particular policy domain, and the extent to which the problems revealed by a potential focusing event are *tangible, obvious harms*. The attributes of potential focusing events that make them worthy of institutional and media attention interact with these features of policy communities, so that differences between policy domains, even those that deal with similar events, will lead to different styles of agenda setting.

Policy Communities, Organization, and Agenda Setting

The nature of the policy community has a direct effect on the influence of focusing events on the institutional agenda. Potential focusing events can stimulate a short-term increase in attention to a problem when there are no advocacy coalitions available to exploit the event for policy change. These events will stimulate some agenda activity that can lead to policy-making activity (not just greater attention) if there is one community that actively seeks change. But beyond this, focusing event influence is a function of the extent of polarization in the domain and the nature of postevent discussions. Simply because an event triggers agenda activity and discussions of policy does not mean that that discussion will deal with key problems or will result in policy change.

No two policy communities are organized the same way. Some communities are very small and handle policy making informally and cooperatively among a well-known set of actors and relationships; other communities are characterized by a large number of actors, highly formal relationships, and intensive competition between groups and actors.

In simplest terms, a policy community can be characterized as more organized or less organized. Highly organized communities include a number of actors and a set of relationships that are well-known to most participants in policy making. Group competition is ongoing; when change happens, it is usually marginal change, rather than broad, sweeping change, because such change would require any group or advocacy coalition to compromise on its core beliefs. When the policy community does change, it usually does so in the wake of a very large shock to the community; such shocks constitute the punctuation in a longer-run equilibrium in policy making (Baumgartner and Jones 1993). Communities with a low degree of organization comprise few actors, and policy-making activity is episodic, incremental, noncompetitive, and generally unremarkable.

Focusing events are much more likely to be important when the policy community that reacts to the event is relatively more organized.

A highly organized policy community is important because the community needs to reach a certain state of organization before there exists
a segment of the community that can take advantage of an event as a
change opportunity. Members of more organized communities are able
to use focusing events to dramatize the need for improved policy, and
therefore can use the opportunity raised by the focusing event to change
relationships and power in the community. Attention to the problem
and actual policy change are more likely to happen when rapid change
shakes a policy community.

Where communities are less well organized, the ability to use
events to improve policy is reduced, even if policy-making activity is
primarily event-driven. This may seem contradictory, but it reveals an
important issue: event-driven policy is not the same as policy making
in which events are used to advance group positions on how to improve
existing policy. Policy communities in which no group competition
exists are so organized because the issues they deal with are lower-
status issues that only gain the attention of nonexpert policy makers
in an emergency. Nonexperts' primary interest is to deal with the
emergency—provide aid, rebuild, and the like—and then move on to
other, more pressing problems. Thus, a great flurry of activity occurs
after an event, but with little influence on policy change.

There are differences between well-organized policy communities
that are important in understanding focusing event politics. In policy
domains where the community is composed of only one advocacy
coalition, events are more likely to be used by members of this single
coalition as part of an internal mobilization strategy that seeks to generate broad public support for policy change. These efforts are unlikely
to attract widespread group opposition, but are more likely to be
greeted with apathy toward or ignorance of the existence of new policy.
This is reflected in the earthquake domain, where an active policy
community is available to take advantage of events and use them to
suggest a need for renewed attention to an ongoing policy problem.
Events may change the domain's agenda from a preevent mode, in
which more abstract or general issues are discussed, to a more event-
oriented discussion of what should be done to mitigate the most recent
event or to prevent a similar recurrence. This pattern also occurs in
the oil spill domain, and to a much lesser extent in the nuclear power
domain. In the latter domains, the process of understanding the meaning of events is much more uncertain, given the need to interpret and
reach a consensus on the damage done by the event.

This style of community is particularly well-suited to distributive
policy making, in which the public is generally uninterested in how
costs and benefits are distributed, and the beneficiaries of the policy

need only meet occasionally to ensure that the largess is efficiently distributed. This is most clearly exemplified by hurricane policy making. As described in chapter 3, Senate and House public works committees are involved in distributing hurricane and flood protection projects. Such distributive policies are relatively easily passed through Congress, but some projects may be more easily approved under the pressure of demands for relief generated by the most recent storm. Such policy making is so routine, and the advocates already so entrenched in Congress, that few interest groups have sprung up to press for aid after hurricanes. Rather, hurricanes simply reinforce existing patterns of distributive public works policy and speed the delivery of funds for aid and for public works projects to repair damage or protect against future storms. These demands dissipate rather quickly as the projects are developed or reconfigured to address the latest disaster. This, coupled with the infrequency of any one area being struck by storms more than once in several years, yields low pressure to create interest groups, while sustaining institutional pressures at the national level to distribute aid. In chapter 3 I show that the hearing record suggests that there is no federal-level policy community of hurricane experts to promote solutions to the problems revealed by hurricanes. The post-hurricane agenda therefore looks much like the preevent agenda; more attention results after a large hurricane, but the substance of posthurricane discussion changes very little. Few new policy initiatives are advanced, and few calls for federal intervention are voiced.

The difference between earthquake and hurricane policy making shows how important expert support is for agenda setting and, ultimately, for policy change. The expert community in the earthquake domain, much of which is employed by government, uses earthquakes to create support for new policy from inside government, in what Cobb, Ross, and Ross (1976) call internal mobilization. This stands in considerable contrast to the nuclear power domain in the 1960s. There the expert community—most of which works in utility companies, nuclear contractors, nuclear engineering departments in universities, and the Atomic Energy Commission—generally supported policy change that promoted, not regulated, nuclear power. This expert community constituted a policy monopoly. Since this monopoly was also in the best position to understand when an important nuclear event occurred and had little interest in publicizing a potential disaster that would contradict its assurances of safety, accidents were unlikely to gain attention outside the expert community.

This was demonstrated by a 1966 near-disaster at the Enrico Fermi nuclear plant near Detroit. The reactor suffered serious damage and, had fissionable materials leaked from the containment structure, well over 100,000 people could have been sickened or killed. The Union of Concerned Scientists (UCS), the most respected of the antinuclear groups, was formed in 1969—two years after the Fermi accident—and was therefore unavailable to provide any alternative story of the near-disaster at Fermi. In contrast to Fermi, the TMI accident shows that such events can mobilize expert antinuclear opinion when this outside expertise is available to be mobilized. Had UCS and other antinuclear groups existed in 1966, the Fermi accident may have stimulated considerably greater antinuclear mobilization, and the collapse of the nuclear policy monopoly may have been hastened.

In chapters 4 and 5 I show that both the oil spill and nuclear power domains are characterized by two sets of similar advocacy coalitions. In each domain there is a status-quo-oriented industry coalition and a change-oriented reform coalition that is usually associated with environmental protection, broadly defined. The debate between these two coalitions turns on whether and to what extent the activity under dispute (oil transportation or nuclear power generation) is injurious to the environment and whether existing regulations and procedures are sufficient to protect the public and the environment from physical or economic harm without creating unreasonable economic burdens.

The debate between these two groups is ongoing and contentious. The conflict between the pro- and antinuclear camps is particularly extreme and ideological. Unlike the oil spill domain, in which the debate centers on the extraction and transportation of oil more than on its suitability as a fuel, the debate in the nuclear power domain goes directly to the issue of whether nuclear power is a safe, economical, and necessary energy source. As a result, and coupled with the low visibility of most nuclear power accidents, accidents tend to have a limited influence on the direction of policy making in the nuclear domain and, indeed, have a very slight influence on the institutional agenda, since the agenda is driven more by the activities of participants in the debate than by particular events.

Thus, the degree to which political conflict overcomes any advantage or disadvantage provided by a focusing event is a function of the visibility and tangibility of an event and of the degree of polarization in the policy community. The most polarized communities will find that events have relatively little influence on the overall trend in policy, as demonstrated in the nuclear power domain. A greater extent of polarization results in a vigorous defense of a coalitions' core beliefs, even in the face of a highly dramatic event. Where politics are somewhat less polarized, as in the oil spill domain, a focusing event will provide one group the opportunity to advance its preferred interpretation of the problem on the agenda. The other group, believing that its position is still legitimate, may need to yield some ground, considering the obvious symbolic power of the event. However, the amount of ground that must be given may not be as great as the postevent imagery and rhetoric may suggest, as some time will pass and memories of the event will fade, giving pro-status-quo groups greater room for negotiation.

The oil spill and the nuclear power domains are considerably polarized between representatives of environmental and public-interest groups, on the one hand, and representatives of industry, on the other. Where there is extreme polarization and extreme disagreement over the harms and meanings of events, focusing events are less likely to have a significant, independent influence on the institutional agenda. This is because the debate over the meaning of oil spills and nuclear power accidents, and over what these industries themselves mean in the broader senses of environmental politics or the public interest, is ongoing. Focusing events will increase mass interest in these problems, particularly in the wake of the largest events, such as the *Exxon Valdez* oil spill and the Three Mile Island nuclear accident. But these events appear to have a smaller influence on policy making than one would imagine, given the flood of news coverage and public interest in their wake. The Three Mile Island accident merely accelerated existing trends away from nuclear power. The *Exxon Valdez* spill directly led to the passage of the Oil Pollution Act of 1990, but that act was rather less stringent than legislation originally introduced after the spill. *Exxon Valdez* simply tipped the balance in a long-standing deadlock, yielding slightly more stringent legislation than had been previously considered. Thus, even large events may not yield long-term shifts in power in these domains. Policy making is usually more incremental and moderate in its breadth and effect than might be supposed in the initial surge of interest after the event.

That any sort of oil spill legislation, after a fourteen-year-long deadlock, was passed reflects the lesser degree of this polarization in oil spills compared with nuclear power policy. Pro- and antinuclear groups are less likely to agree on policy after events. The core beliefs or ideological commitments of these groups are by far the least likely to be compromised or altered by events as the coalitions jockey for political advantage (Sabatier 1988). The oil spill policy community is slightly less polarized because of the nature of the debate over oil spills. Oil spills do not generally call into question broader questions of whether we as a society should use oil for energy or whether oil should be transported by tankers. There are some voices that raise these issues, arguing that oil spills are a symptom of our dependence on fossil fuels and of our wasteful and environmentally damaging lifestyle, but such voices are usually considered as part of the fringe of the debate. Most argument focuses on not whether oil should be extracted and transported, but how, at what cost, and how those costs should be distributed. These costs include liability for spills, costs of greater safety measures, or even uncaptured (at least, from the perspective of the buyer) environmental costs of spilling and cleaning up oil spills. Such a debate is likely to be somewhat less ideological than the debate in the nuclear power domain, considering that it is in neither the oil industry's nor the environmental movement's interest to spill oil, and therefore some common ground or room for compromise is attainable.

The substance of ongoing debate in the domain is also an important clue for understanding how events will influence policy. In the hurricane domain, so much testimony focuses on disaster relief that it seems clear that events may have a short-term agenda effect but little long-term influence on policy. In the earthquake domain, the focus is on technical aspects of the earthquake problem, such as structures, seismology, and other factors that can be examined as part of an overall hazard-reduction mission. Work on these issues continues between events in the earthquake domain, but is elevated on the agenda immediately after events. The substance of policy making in the oil spill and nuclear power domains runs toward liability and responsibility for accidents when events are not on the agenda, and toward cleaning up and dealing with the aftermath of a particular accident when such an event is fresh on the institutional agenda. Policy making in such domains is likely to be highly contentious. Any domain in which policy making focuses on assigning liability—the legal term for blame—is likely to be very contentious and polarized between at least two sets of contenders, including one that wishes to avoid exposure to liability.

Public Participation or Interest in Policy Making

While Americans are well-known for forming groups to promote a wide range of beliefs and interests, public interest in a particular issue can be highly variable. For example, the salience of natural disaster policy is often quite low, both among citizens of hazard-prone areas and among local and regional government officials, whose interest is often occupied by day-to-day problems such as crime, taxes, or economic development issues. Since disaster policy is a low salience issue for most people, this vacuum of interest can only be filled when a professional community forms to study the problem and to press for improved policy, even without much public support. This describes the earthquake domain, where a well-organized and integrated professional community has developed that, when necessary, will press Congress to deal with the hazard at the national level. A parallel community that makes its presence known at congressional hearings has not arisen in the hurricane domain. As a result, when focusing events occur, the primary participants in post-hurricane congressional hearings focus their attention on perceived or real deficiencies in the amount and delivery of federal disaster relief. After hurricanes, attention wanes, and even then the dominant issue on the agenda is problems of disaster relief, not mitigation issues. The lack of sustained public interest in hurricanes means that there is no community, professional or lay, that reacts in a coordinated fashion to large events. In the earthquake domain, there is a community led by professionals, such as scientists and government officials. It is therefore characterized by a style of internal mobilization of the agenda that involves leading the public and its elected representatives to the conclusion that mitigation policy will be, in the long run, a good thing to support.

In the two industrial domains—oil spills and nuclear power accidents—public penetration of the policy process has been much more pronounced. The problems posed by oil and by nuclear power are sufficiently salient to a sufficiently large proportion of the public that groups have formed in the "public interest" to press for more stringent regulation of these industries. Several of these groups were created locally in response to local problems, while others, such as the National Resources Defense Council or the Union of Concerned Scientists, clearly represent a national constituency. The difference between the oil and nuclear case is the extent to which group mobilization and increased group power were event-driven. At the congressional hearing level, one cannot say that antinuclear group activity was primarily event-driven. While the Three Mile Island accident spawned a large but relatively short-lived national antinuclear movement (which rather quickly metamorphosed into an antinuclear-*weapons* movement), most of this movement's political activity was directed toward more direct action, such as public protest rallies. The opening and collapse of the nuclear policy monopoly was due in some part to the efforts of local groups that intervened in the licensing process at plants such as Seabrook (New Hampshire) and Shoreham (Long Island, New York). No particular event mobilized these groups; rather, these groups were mobilized by local concerns and growing fears of the potential dangers of nuclear power.

In the oil domain, local citizens' groups sprung up in direct reaction to particular spills. A citizen's group called Get Oil Out (GOO) was formed in response to the 1969 Santa Barbara Spill. Environmental groups and fishers' organizations—often at odds on other issues—coalesced over the shared threat of the *Exxon Valdez* oil spill. At the national level, groups such as the National Wildlife Fund, the Sierra Club, and the Natural Resources Defense Council seized upon the *Exxon Valdez* accident to promote legislative initiatives, block plans to open the Arctic National Wildlife Reserve to oil exploration, and initiate intensive membership drives.

These differences in public participation patterns help to explain differences in the models of postevent agenda setting in chapters 3 through 5. Ultimately, a focusing event is focal only if an interest group or several groups—some of which may form into advocacy coalitions—are available to react to the event. If no group exists to react to the event, the event will fail to gain more than passing attention. On the other hand, if two well-matched advocacy coalitions are polarized against each other, and engage in vigorous debate over ambiguous events, events will be less focal in that domain.

Event Visibility and the Aggregation of Harms

John Kingdon argues at some length that the focusing power of an event derives from the aggregation of obvious damage. An airplane crash, as noted previously, is much different from a series of fatal automobile accidents, because the airplane crash aggregates its harms in one place at one time.

Even when events aggregate their damage, the visibility and tangibility of damage varies among different types of events. In the simplest terms, the more graphic the damage and the more obvious the event's influence on human populations, the more likely the event will have some focal power. Event visibility here is considered a domain characteristic, based on experience with the largest events in the domain, and not solely as event characteristics.

By this definition, natural disasters are likely to be the most focal, because damage from these events is easily quantified and easily depicted in the news media. When a large natural disaster occurs, the news media flock to the scene and transmit pictures and personal stories of property damage and personal injury. Damage is toted up by insurance companies and government officials. The damage obviously affects people in a very direct way. All these elements make the story surrounding the event readily transmissible to the broader public.

Oil and nuclear accidents[3] are considerably more ambiguous in their effects on people than natural disasters. Earthquakes and hurricanes are directly injurious to people, as measured in deaths, injuries, and property damage. Demands for government action, usually as rapidly delivered disaster relief, are therefore more likely to ensue from the people injured by natural disasters and will be amplified by their elected representatives. The most commonly used measure of the seriousness of an oil spill is the volume of oil spilled. By itself, this is a very rough measure of oil spill damage, even though the statistical models suggest it is the best predictor of news media response to oil spills. The volume of oil spilled does not capture the costs, if any, of a spill to human populations, nor does this measure consider the actual environmental damage done by a spill. A 1,000-gallon spill of bunker oil in an estuary or harbor can be more environmentally damaging than a 100,000-gallon spill of gasoline (which evaporates quickly) in the open ocean. In the nuclear power domain, the measurement of the seriousness of a nuclear power plant accident is even more difficult because there has not yet been an accident at a civilian nuclear power plant that can be demonstrated to have killed anyone in the United States. The proxy I use for the damage done by an event—NRC follow-ups to Abnormal Occurrence Reports—reflects the very real difficulty in assessing how serious an accident was.

Beyond this problem of damage assessment and measurement, oil spills and nuclear power accidents are more likely to be portrayed by partisans in policy debate and the news media as injuries to the environment, not direct injuries to humans. The extent to which the environment is endangered and is fragile is still a point of considerable controversy in this country, and often goes to the core beliefs of the contending advocacy coalitions. Even in the wake of industrial accidents there will be some who argue that the event was less important or injurious than portrayed by environmentalists, the news media, or both. Existing and competitive advocacy coalitions will obviously seek to depict damage in a manner that is most consistent with their policy goals, but the result will be that the depiction of damage done by such events will be considerably more ambiguous than the "objective" damage done by natural disasters.

The difference between oil spills and nuclear power plant accidents turns less, therefore, on objective measures of damage and more on the tangible differences between oil spills and nuclear power plant accidents. After the Santa Barbara and *Exxon Valdez* spills, the news media transmitted many stories and images of oiled shorelines and of oiled and dead birds and sea mammals. These images are vivid and easily conveyed, and serve for most people as obvious indicators that something went very, very wrong in these accidents. By using these symbols, environmental groups provide visual evidence for their claims of environmental damage and corporate recklessness.

The imagery following the most serious nuclear accident, TMI, is much more ambiguous. For many people, the cooling towers of the TMI plant symbolize the event and their fears of nuclear power. Yet the problem with TMI was not with the cooling towers, and, most importantly, there are no images of actual damage to depict this event in symbolically efficient terms. The harms done by TMI were primarily expressed as probabilities, and the discussion of what went wrong with TMI was far more technical and therefore difficult to grasp than the relatively simple stories of Santa Barbara (oil well blowout) or *Exxon Valdez* (ship ran aground).

The importance of this dimension is in the ease with which symbols of these events can be used to expand or contain the issue. Oil spills are literally and figuratively difficult to contain. Nuclear accidents, on the other hand, have proved somewhat more readily confinable. From the industry perspective, it was difficult to prevent the TMI accident from entering media and institutional agendas. This was not because of something inherently dangerous about that particular accident compared with others (after all, one might argue that the Fermi accident was potentially far more dangerous). Rather, it was because of the new regulatory climate that made the containment of the accident so difficult. But even with the widespread knowledge of this accident, these events can be more readily contained because the industry can provide plausible alternative explanations for the accident that can blunt the argument of antinuclear partisans in the wake of the accident. This is not to say that the event can be entirely contained, or that nuclear power plant accidents on the scale of TMI can be shrugged off by the nuclear industry. Rather, it simply means that the relatively weak symbols and images associated with nuclear power accidents thus far in our history suggest that these events are more readily contained and, thus, are less "focal" than large oil spills.

GENERAL COMMENTS ON THE METHOD

A more detailed discussion of the method used in this study, and in particular a discussion of the statistical analysis, is contained in the appendix. In this section I set the stage for the following case studies by providing a general summary of the method I employ.

The case studies that follow concentrate on federal policy making because they are well and consistently documented. While state level policy making is also important, it is beyond the scope of this study.

The events I study—earthquakes, hurricanes, oil spills, and nuclear power plant accidents—took place over a period of 30, 30, 22, and 13 years, respectively. The intent of using long time periods is to ensure that the broad trends of agenda-setting and policy-making activity are considered and, since many of these events are relatively rare, to ensure that the data set is sufficiently large to perform meaningful statistical analyses. Listings of these events, where they occurred, and how much damage they did were obtained primarily from government sources, as supplemented by some privately compiled materials, particularly in the oil spill case, as described in the appendix.

In the models of the media and institutional agendas, the dependent variable is "agenda activity." Agenda activity is composed of two elements. The first is the change in attention to the problem (earthquakes generally, for example) in the two years after the event, compared with the two years before it. This is measured by using the *New York Times Index*, and bill introductions and mentions of the problem in congressional hearings. The second element is the agenda *density* of an issue, which is computed as the amount of discussion (news stories or testimony) of the problem *attributable to the event under scrutiny* divided by all discussion of the problem. Thus, an event with an agenda density of 0.75 would mean that 75 percent of all discussion of the issue in the two-year period after the event would be attributable to the particular event. The importance of this measure is made clear in chapter 3, where the bunching effect of hurricanes makes it difficult to attribute agenda change, by itself, to particular events.

The independent variables are relatively straightforward, and all data sources are documented in the appendix. The statistical analysis is only part of the story, however; it serves as a starting point for a discussion of why some events emerged as more focal than others, and why the domains seem to differ from each other in important and sometimes unexpected ways.

CONCLUSION

In this chapter I introduce a framework for the study of focusing events. This framework is used to select the events and the variables considered in the following chapters. But this framework, or model, like most models in the social sciences, cannot explain all the variation in a particular domain. In the chapters that follow, I use this framework to specify empirical models that are tested with data on agenda status, group activity, news coverage, and the harms done by these events. The framework also provides some direction for seeking to understand why particular events are most focal and how the focusing effect of events can vary across ostensibly similar policy domains.

3

Natural Disasters as Focusing Events

Natural disasters are among humanity's most expensive, deadliest, and feared events. Nature poses substantial dangers to human populations from earthquakes, hurricanes, tornadoes, flash floods, droughts, heat waves, ice storms, wildfires, and other natural phenomena. The economic toll of these disasters is quite large, and although modern technology can mitigate property damage and loss of life, no amount of human effort can eliminate natural disasters. The number of deaths from individual disasters in the United States is declining, and while private charities and the government provide disaster relief, the economic toll from natural disasters is large and growing. Annually, natural disasters cause about $20 billion in direct damage and $30 to $35 billion in indirect damage. Just two disasters, Hurricane Hugo and the Loma Prieta earthquake, did over $15 billion in direct damage. Improvements in building, planning, and hazard-reduction programs are largely offset each year by the increasing number of people and value of property in high-risk areas (Burby and Dalton 1993, 229; National Research Council 1991). While aggregate statistics reflect substantial damage from these events, they cannot measure the individual suffering that results from the loss of or injury to one's family, friends, or home in natural disasters.

Earthquakes and hurricanes are particularly damaging disasters. In the period of this study there were relatively few earthquake fatalities, but property damage from earthquakes in the data set is substantial, ranging from just over $1 million to approximately $6 billion in 1990 dollars. The damage done to infrastructure is highly disruptive to a community, taking months to repair and leaving water shortages, sanitation problems, power outages, broken gas lines, and traffic congestion in its wake.

Strong hurricanes also do substantial damage to property and infrastructure, and when preparations are insufficient or when the storm is particularly severe, they can lead to loss of life. Hurricane winds do considerable damage, but damage is also done along the shoreline by the storm surge, the wall of water propelled by wind and waves. Hurricanes are defined as tropical storms with winds exceeding 74 miles per hour.[1] The smallest hurricanes—Category 1 on the Saffir/ Simpson scale—are relatively minor, with winds of between 74 and 95 miles per hour and a storm surge of about 4 to 5 feet. A Category 5 storm, on the other hand, packs winds of over 155 miles per hour, with a storm surge along the coastline of greater than 18 feet. The only Category 5 storm in this study is Hurricane Camille, which struck the Louisiana Gulf Coast in 1969 and did substantial damage to coastal and island areas.[2]

Hurricanes tend to strike most often in the Southeastern United States. States at greatest risk include the Carolinas, Georgia, Florida, Alabama, Mississippi, Louisiana, and Texas. When storms turn up the Eastern Seaboard, states from Florida to Maine can be affected, sometimes severely. Long Island (New York) and New England, extending eastward into the Atlantic ocean, tend to bear the brunt of such storms. Hurricane Gloria in 1985, for example, barely brushed New Jersey but did substantial damage to Long Island.

The most damaging earthquakes in this study struck California and Alaska, but at least 39 states are also subject to earthquakes (Federal Emergency Management Agency 1992). Historic earthquakes have struck the Cape Ann area of Massachusetts in the 1700s, Charleston, South Carolina, in 1889, and the Puget Sound region of Washington State in 1948 and 1965. Perhaps the greatest series of earthquakes felt in North America struck in 1811 and 1812 near New Madrid, Missouri, when the area was sparsely populated. Earthquakes of similar magnitude today could do substantial damage to St. Louis, Memphis, and their environs. While the threat of earthquakes in areas outside California is well-known to professionals in this field, public appreciation of the dangers of earthquakes outside California is relatively low.

The economic and physical toll of natural disasters has led to real or perceived public demands for disaster relief as matters of charity and equity. This demand is met by private relief agencies such as the Salvation Army and the Red Cross, and by state and federal governments. More recently, the federal government has begun to realize that the most effective way to reduce postdisaster costs and suffering is through encouraging sound disaster-mitigation policy at the local level.

Most public officials acknowledge that the public, in a diffuse and vague way, demands federal, state, and local disaster-relief programs, particularly when many people have been directly victimized. However, there are no active, broad-based public-interest groups pressing for government action to prevent damage from disasters. Indeed, some citizens and local governments often resist costly land-use planning and building code measures to prevent harm from a generally unpredictable hazard (May and Birkland 1994). As a result, there is no obvious constituency for policy entrepreneurs to draw upon to advance disaster-prevention and mitigation programs, leading, in turn, to few policy entrepreneurs who persist in working to keep disaster-mitigation and damage-prevention issues high on the agenda. In the earthquake domain there are some experts to provide needed expertise between major earthquakes and to deliver what might be called "I told you so" messages in hearings and other forums. In the hurricane domain, on the other hand, political entrepreneurs are sparse. The "disaster problem" thus languishes near the bottom of national, state, and local priorities until the problem is elevated on the agenda, not by political activity, a change in indicators, or some political perturbation, but by a completely exogenous and largely unpredictable event.

In this chapter I assess the influence of natural disasters on the congressional[3] and media agenda. The first part of this analysis is a review of the political context in which disaster policy is made. I then introduce an empirical analysis of agenda dynamics in these two types of disasters. These models, while broadly supporting the theory, reveal important differences in the agenda behavior of earthquakes and hurricanes. I discuss these differences in detail and consider how the composition of the policy community influences the agenda dynamics of a policy domain. I conclude with an assessment of the success of the theory of focusing events, considering the empirical analysis.

THE POLICY AND POLITICAL CONTEXT
OF NATURAL DISASTERS

The federal government's efforts to alleviate suffering in the wake of disasters traditionally concentrate on disaster relief.[4] The Disaster Relief Act of 1950 (PL 81-875) replaced ad hoc, event-specific aid packages with general disaster relief law. Subsequent legislation has often been event-specific and, as typifies distributive policy (Ripley and Franklin 1984), is characterized by logrolling and accommodation of particular areas' needs. May (1985, 21) notes that not only was such logrolling predicated on potential future disasters, but it was also based on past disasters. Aid provisions retroactive to prior disasters were often written into new relief measures to ensure broader support.

Before the National Earthquake Hazards Reduction Act (NEHRA) of 1977, which created the National Earthquake Hazards Reduction Program (NEHRP), no coherent federal policy existed to encourage research on and implementation of ways to reduce earthquake losses. Except for the mitigation-oriented elements of the national floodplain and flood insurance program, there is little mitigation-oriented federal policy and none concerning hurricanes per se. The lack of preventive disaster policy can be attributed to the routine pressures on government officials and citizens to deal with many other problems that are much more salient until there is a catastrophic disaster (May 1985, 8; Rossi, Wright, and Weber-Burdin 1982). Once a disaster strikes, the immediate interest of local officials and residents is in being quickly granted aid, rather than dealing with prospective events. Soon after the event, interest in the event subsides, and disaster policy returns to its prior status as the province of technical experts charged with analyzing, predicting, and providing relief after disasters. Even then, technical expertise is far less important in policy dealing with hurricanes, where there is no program comparable to the National Earthquake Hazard Reduction Program and, therefore, no coherent policy community at the national level. Rather than a coherent national program to deal with hurricanes, there are at least six federal statutes that indirectly influence federal response toward hurricanes: the Coastal Zone Management Act, The National Flood Insurance Act, the Flood Disaster Protection Act, the Stafford Disaster Relief and Emergency Assistance Act, Federal Flood Control Acts, and the Coastal Barrier Resources Act. In particular, the Coastal Barrier Resources Act of 1982 is a broader program that has reduced, to some degree, the exposure of people and property to the hurricane hazard by reducing coastal development. The National Flood Insurance Program (NFIP) contains important mitigation requirements as conditions of eligibility for flood insurance. This is important to residents of hurricane areas, as flooding from the storm surge and from heavy rains does the most damage in these storms. However, none of these statutes address the hurricane problem directly, but, rather, touch on the problem as part of broader issues such as flood control or barrier island conservation.

The challenge for policy makers who wish to raise awareness of and mitigate natural hazards is to gain the attention of potential victims and local officials before the disaster strikes. This challenge is compounded by the lack of broadly supported citizens' groups that are generally mobilized by the natural disaster threat (Stallings 1995). Peter May calls low-salience issues with low levels of public mobilization, such as natural disasters, "policies without publics" that show "limited development of interest groups, usually restricted to technical and scientific communities" (May 1990, 190). Thus, in the aftermath of a disaster, there are no public-interest groups that mobilize to press for improved disaster-mitigation policies.

There are few if any publics in the earthquake or hurricane domains, particularly in the predisaster period, that organize based on the potential of great future harms if government fails to act in a particular way. The only organized interests found in the two domains studied here are technical and scientific experts who deal with earthquakes. As shown later in this chapter, such expertise is far less important in the hurricane domain than in the earthquake domain. The nature and composition of natural disaster policy communities may change for a short period immediately after an event, as victims and their representatives enter and exit the community. Over the long run the composition of the policy community does not change significantly, and the problem returns to its previous low-salience status.

In summary, disaster policy is the province of technical experts or legislative specialists when the problem is least salient to elected officials and the public. When a disaster forces the issue up the agenda, disaster policy deals with deficiencies in the delivery of relief and relegates relief agencies in the federal government to a defensive, subordinate role immediately after a disaster. Disaster-relief policy ultimately responds to an event by advancing policy that deals retrospectively with deficiencies in the delivery of disaster relief, while rarely if ever dealing prospectively with future disasters. Generals are said to be ready to fight the last war; disaster policy seems to be geared to respond to the last disaster.

AGENDA DYNAMICS IN THE EARTHQUAKE AND HURRICANE DOMAINS

To understand the dynamics of agenda setting after earthquakes and hurricanes, I model the influence of event attributes and their subsequent political attributes on the news agenda and on the congressional agenda. In the models, individual events are the units of analysis. The dependent variables of interest are measures of news and institutional "agenda activity." The term "activity" is used because this variable considers more than simply agenda change. Agenda activity is the rate of agenda change times the agenda density of an event. Agenda change is measured by counting the absolute numbers of bills introduced and testimony delivered to congressional committees in the two-year periods before and after focusing events, and calculating the rate of change. The rate of news change is similarly constructed, using the level of coverage of the issue in the *New York Times Index*.

Agenda density measures the extent to which a particular event dominates the agenda. It is computed by dividing the number of witnesses that testified about a particular event in the two-year period after the event by the total number of witnesses discussing the disaster type in the same period. Thus, the theoretical range of the density variable is from 0.0 to 1.0. The density variable serves as a discount factor, so that events that simply coincide with agenda change do not carry the same weight as events that are more directly related to agenda change. The most important events, of course, are those that dominate the agenda and lead to a great deal of agenda change. The density variable is particularly important in the hurricane domain, where events tend to group together, making it difficult to isolate an event's effect on the agenda without the density variable. This effect, and additional information on the variables, is discussed in greater detail in the appendix.

Agenda Response to the Immediate Event

Table 3-1 shows the relationships between immediate event attributes and news and congressional agenda activity. These relationships work as expected, and in terms of the congressional agenda, the domains are roughly parallel; the extent of damage and deaths is more strongly correlated with congressional agenda activity than rarity and scope in both earthquakes and hurricanes. Yet the rarity and scope of hurricanes are considerably more important in setting that agenda than they are

TABLE 3-1   Event Attribute Models

Dependent Variables	*Correlation Coefficients*			
	News Agenda Activity		*Congressional Agenda Activity*	
	Earthquakes	*Hurricanes*	*Earthquakes*	*Hurricanes*
Damage	0.829	0.304	0.916	0.736
Deaths	0.723	0.154	0.912	0.700
Rarity	0.426	0.477	0.351	0.582
Scope	0.281	0.406	0.123	0.283
N	38	25	38	25
	Regression Results:[a]			
Adjusted R^2	0.680	0.277	0.876	0.812
F	27.163	4.058	87.915	35.565
p	0.000	0.020	0.000	0.000

[a] Dependent variables are news and institutional activity, respectively. Regression model uses interaction term between damage and deaths. Variables are transformed to meet the requirements of OLS regression. Variables are defined in the text and in the appendix.

in setting the earthquake agenda. The damage done by earthquakes is more important than that done by hurricanes.

News activity is highly related to the level of deaths and damage in earthquakes, while these relationships are weaker in hurricanes. These differences can be laid to the nature of the damage done by these disasters. In an earthquake, damage tends to be concentrated in a fairly compact geographic area. The damage done by earthquakes is dramatic and very graphic: bridges collapse, buildings tumble, and fires sparked by the earthquake burn entire blocks. Among the most pervasive images of the 1989 Loma Prieta and 1994 Northridge earthquakes were images of collapsed freeways and of fires, often in the most incongruous contexts, as when gas and water lines burst in the Northridge earthquake, yielding gas fires in the midst of rushing water from broken mains. Hurricane damage, on the other hand, tends to be widely dispersed across a broad geographic area and, unless the storm is of unusually great magnitude, the damage tends to be less graphic than that caused by earthquakes. Inland damage usually consists of broken windows, flooding, and downed trees and utility lines. This sort of damage is usually expected, is often less than originally feared, and is generally part of the routine of living in hurricane areas. In sum, earthquake damage and deaths are, in news terms, more dramatic than damage that results from hurricanes.

POSTEVENT POLITICS AND THE CONGRESSIONAL AGENDA

The influence of postevent political attributes of earthquakes and hurricanes on the congressional agenda is summarized in Table 3-2. Change in the amount of news coverage of an event and the density of that coverage are both important determinants of congressional agenda activity in the earthquake domain, suggesting that members of the policy community are influenced by the extent of news coverage of earthquakes. The level of news density is important in setting the hurricane agenda, but news change is less important because of the bunching effect of hurricanes. This phenomenon—due in large part to the seasonal nature of hurricanes—makes the influence of one particular event difficult to discern when there are several events on the agenda. A more useful comparison between the two domains, then, is on the density of news coverage, since this variable considers the extent to which a particular event dominates the news agenda.[5] This news coverage is an important determinant in the postevent institutional agenda because, after disasters, the news media are the primary conduits of information from the disaster scene to decision makers. The major national newspapers, such as the *New York Times* or *Washington*

TABLE 3-2   Political Model of the Congressional Agenda

	Standardized Regression Coefficients	
Dependent variable:	Congressional Agenda Activity	
	Earthquakes	Hurricanes
News Change	0.451**	−0.032
News Density	0.372**	0.696**
Mobilization	0.307**	0.357*
Scope	0.028	−0.091
Tone	−0.380**	0.109
N	38	25
Adjusted R^2	0.633	0.371
F	13.746	3.836
p	0.000	0.014

$*p<.05$ $**p<.01$

Post, are the major sources of disaster information for decision makers in Washington D.C. (Smith 1992).

The mean tone of testimony in the domain—that is, the extent to which current policy toward a hazard is supported or criticized by a witness—is important in the earthquake domain, but not in the hurricane domain. As I will show, the overall witness list for hurricane hearings is dominated by witnesses who testify about particular events, whose testimony is generally critical of existing policy, whose testimony centers on disaster relief, and who rarely appear to discuss the hazard between storms. In the earthquake domain there is greater variation in witnesses' attitudes toward current policy. There the policy type discussed in event-driven testimony differs from policies considered in routine testimony, while in the hurricane domain there is no difference between event-driven and other testimony. Thus, in the earthquake domain an event leads to more critical analysis, compared with testimony that is unrelated to an event. This criticism leads to greater congressional agenda activity as policy makers seek to correct problems in existing policy.

The mobilization variable measures the extent to which political conflict increases after a focusing event. This variable is the ratio of prochange groups that testify in the two-year period after an event to the number of pro-status-quo testifiers. More focal events lead to a greater political imbalance between prochange and pro-status-quo interest groups, which can lead to greater institutional attention to the issue as congressional partisans and policy brokers seek to advance the issues or seek a resolution to conflict. I assess whether a group type is prochange or pro-status-quo by calculating the mean tone of testimony offered by members of the group type in question over the period of the study. Group types with a mean testimony tone of less than zero throughout the period of the study are assumed to be pro-change, while group types with a mean tone of greater than zero are pro-status-quo. In both domains, political conflict over policy plays an important role in congressional agenda activity, suggesting that events do indeed mobilize prochange witnesses and that their activity is an important determinant of congressional agenda activity.

Finally, scope is not a statistically significant variable in the models. However, as shown in Table 3-1, the scope of events is correlated with agenda activity, particularly in news coverage. This suggests that scope at best indirectly affects news coverage, which in turn influences congressional agenda activity.

The analysis reveals important differences between the two domains. First, the bivariate models suggest that the extent of damage and deaths after an earthquake is more highly correlated with news and congressional agenda activity than is found in hurricanes. This is particularly true of news activity, which is much more highly correlated with damage and deaths after earthquakes than after hurricanes. Second, in the regression models all the variables, except for scope, are significant and behave as hypothesized in the earthquake model, while only the news density and pro/antichange variables are significant in the hurricane models. Considering the correlation results, we might conclude that scope is more important in the hurricane domain than in the earthquake domain. However, the regression coefficients are nonsignificant and it appears that scope, by itself, is not an important contributor to the focusing power of events.

Professional Mobilization after Natural Disasters

The framework introduced in chapter 2 was developed on the assumption that while natural disasters and other sudden-onset disasters, like industrial accidents, may differ in some ways, they are sufficiently similar that focusing event politics would be similar across domains. The results of the analysis suggest that the differences may be at least as interesting as the similarities. These differences can be explained by reviewing research on natural disasters, risk, and the response of institutions to unexpected events. Such an analysis begins with recognizing that there are differences in how people perceive risk and natural hazards.

Psychological research on risk shows "that people do not define risk solely as the expected number of deaths or injuries per unit time. [P]eople also rank risks based on how well the process in question is understood, how equitably the danger is distributed, how well individuals can control their exposure, and whether risk is assumed voluntarily" (Morgan 1993, 35). Morgan notes that experimental psychologists Baruch Fischoff, Paul Slovic and Sarah Lichtenstein (e.g. Fischoff, Slovic, and Lichtenstein 1979a; Fischoff, Slovic, and Lichtenstein 1979b; Slovic, Lichtenstein, and Fischoff 1984) categorize risk factors in three groups. "The first is basically an event's degree of dreadfulness (as determined by such features as the scale of its effects and the degree to which it affects 'innocent' bystanders). The second is a measure of how well the risk is understood, and the third is the number of people exposed" (Morgan 1993, 35). Risk analysts have found that "risks carrying a high level of 'dread,' for example, provoke more calls for government intervention than do some more workaday risks that actually cause more deaths than injuries" (ibid.).

This research helps to explain the differences between earthquakes and hurricanes. The degree of dreadfulness and the extent to which the risk is understood are particularly important. Both earthquakes and hurricanes are "dreadful" because, when they strike in populated areas, they affect many people at once. Some of these people are very directly influenced—they are killed, injured, lose family and friends to death or injury, or suffer economic loss—and therefore are broadly viewed as "innocent" bystanders who suffer through little or no fault of their own. Aside from the few people who ignore disaster warnings (those who drown while surfing a hurricane's storm surge, or get too close to a beach to view a tsunami, for example), most disaster victims evoke sympathy from others, and disasters often lead to offers of humanitarian aid from charities and other communities.

Earthquakes may be more dreadful than hurricanes because more is known about hurricanes than about earthquakes. The physical action of damaging coastal storms has been well-known in the coastal United States for many years. The prediction of hurricanes has improved considerably since the 1940s. Before satellite weather maps and improved meteorological technology, hurricanes would often strike with relatively little warning. In the early 1960s improved technology allowed forecasters to find, track, and predict the time of landfall of dangerous storms. The results of this knowledge, as well as improved scientific knowledge of storm surge and wind effects, is remarkable. The disastrous 1938 hurricane that devastated Long Island and New England killed 600 people, largely because hurricane forecasting was primitive, communications between communities in the path of the storm were knocked out, and because the human and institutional adjustments to such storms were still underdeveloped. Hurricane Camille (1969), the deadliest storm in this study, killed 296 people, a considerable improvement over the 1938 toll, but still an unacceptably large toll to most people. Hurricane Hugo, a very powerful category three storm, killed 60 people, while doing more damage than any hurricane since Camille. In most industrialized nations, the trend in natural disasters is lower death tolls as human adjustment to the hazard improves, but higher property damage as more development occurs in the most hazard-prone areas.

Earthquakes are also becoming more damaging, but are also killing fewer people relative to property damage because of improvements in building codes, better knowledge of land-use practices, and more disaster-aware publics in areas that are most prone to earthquakes, particularly in California. Overall, knowledge of earthquake mechanics and how human populations should prepare for earthquakes is still lower than our knowledge of hurricanes. It has been known for some time that most damage done by hurricanes is done by wind and storm surge action, and that the damage done by earthquakes is due to ground shaking, ground failure, or both, leading to structural failure. But structural engineering for earthquakes is not a static science. Sometimes earthquakes behave rather differently than expected, confounding the best efforts of scientists and engineers. The San Fernando earthquake, while only moderately strong in Richter magnitude, caused ground motion in some places that was greater than had ever been recorded in an earthquake. The 1994 Northridge earthquake caused considerable damage in particular to steel frame structures built to what were once the most advanced standards, developed as they were after the 1971 San Fernando earthquake (Housner 1994). Clearly, when older "state of the art" practices and codes are shown to be insufficient, improved practices and standards must be developed and implemented if we are to improve our preparation for powerful earthquakes. Earthquakes often trigger new rounds of research and standards adoption.

There is also less knowledge of where and when earthquakes will strike compared with hurricanes. Residents of the Gulf and Atlantic coasts know that they live with the possibility of hurricanes; the risk is greatest in the eastern Gulf and southeastern Atlantic coasts, and during a particular season. The earthquake threat is less specific: along with the most commonly perceived earthquake-prone areas—such as California and Alaska—the Midwest, the Charleston, South Carolina area, and the Boston area are also subject to the threat. But unlike hurricanes, which can be anticipated during hurricane season, earthquakes can strike any time. When they do strike, they sometimes are the result of movement on an undiscovered fault, as when the Northridge earthquake struck on a relatively deep blind-thrust fault (Housner 1994, 13). Finally, while hurricanes provide some lead time to prepare for the storm, earthquakes provide no such lead time, thereby making them even more frightening. Any preparations for earthquakes must be made well before such an event strikes, whereas the lead time before a hurricane gives people the sense that they can "do something" to protect themselves, even if they have been lax in their preparations before the disaster.

None of this is meant to suggest that hurricanes are less dangerous than earthquakes. Rather, this suggests that popular risk calculations make earthquakes somewhat more dreadful and thus somewhat more dramatic news stories than hurricanes. The result is that journalists writing about hurricanes use another hook for their stories besides deaths and damage per se. Two possible story hooks include the rarity and scope of a disaster.

In the hurricane case, there is a considerable difference between the media model and the congressional agenda. Disaster impact is very important to the congressional hurricane agenda, suggesting that even when the news media pay less attention to disaster impact, congressional committees pay attention to disaster impact because of the effect on residents of local congressional districts. But rarity is also important, suggesting, again, that exceptionality influences congressional attention to hurricanes, while the rarity of an event does not influence congressional attention to earthquakes. Again, this may be because earthquakes tend to cluster less than hurricanes, and because the greater dreadfulness of earthquakes may result in greater congressional attention regardless of the span of time between events.

The higher priority placed on science in addressing earthquakes compared with hurricanes is reflected by the small, less visible, and yet more balkanized scientific community dealing with hurricanes. This community concentrates primarily on weather forecasting but also includes wind engineers, structural engineers, and theoretical meteorologists. The earthquake community is comparatively larger and is centered on earth science and hazard reduction through improved engineering and technical knowledge. That the greatest attention in the hurricane domain is paid to weather forecasting, a relatively mature discipline, suggests that there is little institutional pressure or interest group advocacy to learn more about potential engineering responses to hurricanes. This is because there appears to be a perception that more scientific knowledge is needed to mitigate the earthquake hazard than hurricanes.

If the differences between the domains are as described, there should be evidence of the greater importance of scientific and technical expertise in policy making in the earthquake domain and less such expertise in the hurricane domain. There are three ways to explore the importance of scientific and technical expertise in these domains. The first is to examine the nature of the committees that hear the most testimony in the policy community. A community in which testimony is delivered most often to scientific and technical committees is substantially different from a community in which most testimony is delivered to committees concerned with public works. The second way is to look at the types of groups that appear most often before congressional committees in their respective domains. Finally, we can see which policy entrepreneurs are most important in each domain, both to understand the extent to which policy entrepreneurship is important in a domain and to understand the primary concerns on policy entrepreneurs' agendas.

The Influence of Focusing Events on the Policy Community

The earthquake and hurricane cases show that focusing events change the contours of policy communities. In particular, the postevent agenda in the community changes and decision makers and policy entrepreneurs are more active after a focusing event than they were before the event. However, there are important differences between the earthquake and hurricane policy communities that are highlighted by examining postdisaster agenda setting.

Postevent politics can differ from "normal" politics more removed from events in four ways. These differences are based on the level of activity in Congress, the tone of the testimony offered in response to an event, and differences in the predominant issue on the agenda before and after large events. These differences are reflected in Tables 3-3A and 3-3B.

First, there is more testimony centered on an event than testimony that is not centered on an event in both the earthquake and hurricane domains. By "centered" I mean that the testimony in question is about, in a substantial way, a particular disaster. A witness called before a hearing to discuss the seismic safety of hospitals overall is not offering testimony centered on an event, while a witness testifying about the seismic safety of particular hospitals after the San Fernando earthquake of 1971 is delivering testimony centered on the San Fernando event. The mere mention of an event as an example does not qualify testimony as "centered." The results confirm that, in broad terms, there is greater activity in the policy community after a focusing event. This is not to say that all testimony in a domain is event-centered, as seen in the earthquake domain, but that there is a clear tendency in both domains to hear from more witnesses when an event is high on the agenda.

Second, because a considerable amount of dissatisfaction with current policy is revealed and intensified by an event (Kemp 1984), one might reasonably expect that the tone of the testimony delivered in

TABLE 3-3A   Testimony, Field Hearings, and Testimony Centered on Earthquakes

Hearing Type		Testimony Type		
		Centered on an Event	All Others	Total
Field	Mean tone[a]	−0.462	−0.250	−0.430
	N	266	48	314
	Modal Policy[b]	Disaster Relief	Earth Science	Disaster Relief
Washington	Mean tone	−0.186	−0.019	−0.047
	N	43	211	254
	Modal Policy	Disaster Relief	NEHRP	NEHRP
Total	Mean tone	−0.424	−0.062	−0.259
	N	309	259	568
	Modal Policy	Disaster Relief	NEHRP	Disaster Relief

Notes:
For total analysis of variance on mean tone: $F_{3,564}$=10.584, p=0.000
For distribution of hearing type and testimony type, Chi-squared with 1 df = 259.09, p<0.001
[a]Tone is a measure of attitudes toward existing policy, where +1 indicates general support for existing policy, −1 indicates opposition to existing policy, and 0 is neutral.
[b]Policy type is the predominant topic discussed by the witness in a congressional hearing, based on the review of testimony in each domain.

response to an event will be more negative than when testimony is not centered on a particular event. However, this is true only in testimony offered on earthquakes. In all instances of testimony in both domains the mean tone is negative, an unsurprising result as Congress is generally unmotivated to hold oversight hearings when policy is generally believed to be working well. Testimony centered on events is significantly more negative in the earthquake domain compared to nonevent testimony, while testimony in the hurricane domain is uniformly negative regardless of whether or not an event is on the agenda. This result confirms the results of the regression models. They showed that testimony tone after a hurricane is unrelated to congressional agenda activity, while the negative tone of postearthquake testimony is an important trigger of congressional agenda activity.

While hurricanes trigger more testimony, they do not result in a statistically significant change in the mean tone of testimony. Scientific and technical experts who specialize in hurricanes are considerably less active in discussions of federal policy. The result is that testimony

TABLE 3-3B   Testimony, Field Hearings, and Testimony Centered on Hurricanes

		Testimony Type		
Hearing Type		Centered on an Event	All Others	Total
Field	Mean tone	−0.254	−0.243	−0.252
	N	276	37	313
Washington	Mean tone	−0.304	−0.225	−0.247
	N	79	200	279
Total	Mean tone	−0.265	−0.228	−0.250
	N	355	237	592

Notes:
Modal policy in all cells is Disaster Relief
For total analysis of variance on mean tone: $F_{3,588}=0.148$ p=0.931
For distribution of hearing type and testimony type, Chi-squared with 1 df = 220.20, p<0.001
[a]Tone is a measure of attitudes toward existing policy, where +1 indicates general support for existing policy, −1 indicates opposition to existing policy, and 0 is neutral.

in the hurricane domain is overwhelmingly delivered in the wake of disasters, is dominated by relief issues, has no professional community to act as a moderating influence, and is therefore overwhelmingly and consistently negative.

By contrast, earthquakes lead to changes both in amount of testimony and in the mean tone of testimony delivered at hearings. This difference is due to the existence of an active policy community that deals with earthquakes and the virtual absence of a similar community in the hurricane domain. The tone of testimony delivered between events in the earthquake community tends to be less negative, as a great deal of scientific testimony in general is offered that is neutral in tone. While members of the earthquake community may disagree at some level over the appropriate course of policy, scientific testimony is less negative than overall testimony delivered in the wake of a disaster. Disaster-related testimony is dominated by victims and their representatives rather than by professionals in the domain. Immediately after an earthquake, these professionals find their testimony overshadowed by complaints about disaster relief.

None of this is to say that scientific testimony is unaffected by large events. Some members of the scientific community also evaluate existing policy negatively, but the policy that scientists evaluate tends to focus on scientific issues rather than disaster relief. The predominant topic of postdisaster discussion, regardless of the size of the scientific community, is disaster relief, however, and such testimony clearly overshadows all other testimony, regardless of its source.

Finally, only in the earthquake domain does the type of policy that dominates the agenda differ between event and nonevent testimony. The modal policy type in the earthquake domain when a particular disaster is not prominent on the agenda revolves around scientific and technical issues in the domain, either earth science generally or discussion of the proposed or (after 1977) enacted National Earthquake Hazards Reduction Program (NEHRP). There is no equivalent, comprehensive, hazard-specific program created by statute related to hurricanes. While there is a hurricane program at FEMA, this program is not created by law, and therefore carries less weight than the NEHRP. There is a considerable amount of scientific work in the hurricane domain, such as weather forecasting and modeling and understanding the mechanics of the coastal storm surge. But there is no scientific community as large as that in the earthquake domain that is reflected in federal hurricane policy making, in large part due to the lack of the centralizing influence of a legislatively mandated program akin to the NEHRP. Thus, as with tone, the type of policy varies little between testimony centered and not centered on events.

ASSESSING POLICY COMMUNITY RESPONSE TO FOCUSING EVENTS

The theory of focusing events and agenda change rests on an assumption that decision makers and policy entrepreneurs are more active in response to focusing events than during periods between events. The analyses of the earthquake and hurricane communities suggest that there is a community of policy entrepreneurs who deal with earthquakes, while there appear to be fewer policy entrepreneurs in hurricane policy. To highlight the differences, Tables 3-4A and 3-4B show that there is considerably greater decision-maker and policy-entrepreneur activity between earthquake events, while there is roughly the same between-event and postevent decision-maker and policy-entrepreneur activity dealing with hurricanes. In short, the earthquake policy community is much more important and active in that domain; there appears to be a very tenuous policy community that deals with hurricanes.

Overall, policy entrepreneurs and decision makers in the earthquake community are more likely to testify in the abstract, rather than in response to a particular event; in contrast, decision makers and policy entrepreneurs are overwhelmingly more active in response to hurricanes. Again, this is evidence of a larger and more active earth-

TABLE 3-4A   Decision Maker and Policy Entrepreneur Activity: Earthquakes

Testimony	Decision Makers[a]		Policy Entrepreneurs[b]	
	Centered on Event	Not Centered	Centered on Event	Not Centered
N of witnesses	72	129	61	141
Mean Tone[c]	0.222	0.163	−0.131	0.050
t		0.492		−1.111
p (one tailed)		0.312		0.134

[a]Decision makers are witnesses in a policy-making role in the federal legislative or executive branch.
[b]Policy entrepreneurs are witnesses who appeared two or more times in hearings in their respective fields.
[c]Tone is attitude toward current policy, where −1 indicates dissatisfaction with current policy and +1 indicates satisfaction with policy.

quake policy community than exists in the hurricane domain, where policy-entrepreneur and decision-maker testimony is more likely to be centered on particular events.

In both domains, there is also evidence of a policy monopoly seeking to defend current policy, and to defend its position vis a vis opponents who are more likely to be dissatisfied with current policy at the time of the earthquake or hurricane. In both domains, when decision makers discuss particular events, their attitudes toward policy are much more positive than those of policy entrepreneurs, and are also

TABLE 3-4B   Decision Maker and Policy Entrepreneur Activity: Hurricanes

Testimony	Decision Makers[a]		Policy Entrepreneurs[b]	
	Centered on Event	Not Centered	Centered on Event	Not Centered
N of witnesses	96	101	59	56
Mean Tone[c]	0.073	−0.119	−0.322	−0.375
t		1.330		0.347
p (one tailed)		0.093		0.365

[a] Decision makers are witnesses in a policy-making role in the federal legislative or executive branch.
[b]Policy entrepreneurs are witnesses who appeared two or more times in hearings in their respective fields.
[c]Tone is attitude toward current policy, where −1 indicates dissatisfaction with current policy and +1 indicates satisfaction with policy.

more positive than their own attitudes toward policy when particular events are not the center of their testimony. The gap between decision makers and policy entrepreneurs is particularly pronounced in the hurricane domain. These differences in the hurricane domain appear to turn on federal decision makers' defense of existing disaster-relief policy, which must follow procedures to deliver aid as fairly and effectively as possible. Some of these rules are perceived by local governmental officials and disaster-relief groups as arbitrary, inefficient, or "bureaucratic." There is thus a built-in difference between the interests of relief delivery agencies and the representatives of victims. This dynamic is also reflected in the earthquake domain. In the interevent period, there are more negative voices among decision makers than among policy entrepreneurs who call for improvements in federal policy. This is additional evidence of the existence of an ongoing policy community that is concerned with more than the delivery of disaster relief.

To summarize, the earthquake domain has an active policy community that is mobilized during postevent periods and continues activity between such events. The hurricane community has no coherent scientific community that participates in congressional hearings between hurricanes. Without the participation of the scientific community, interest in the hurricane problem does increase in the wake of events, but this interest is centered almost solely on disaster relief and virtually disappears as the memory of the storm fades.

The Congressional Committee Environment

The results of the analyses thus far suggest that there are important differences between earthquake and hurricane policy making. The first place to look for these differences is in the type of committees or subcommittees that assume jurisdiction over these disasters.

House and Senate public works committees dominate the hurricane issue, hearing 63.8 percent of the testimony delivered on this issue. By contrast, the top two committees in the earthquake domain, the House Science, Space and Technology Committee and the Senate Commerce, Science and Transportation Committee, heard 38.6 percent of the testimony heard in this domain. These patterns reflect the reasons for the near-exclusive orientation toward disaster relief in the hurricane domain, on the one hand, and the mixed hazard-reduction and disaster-relief agendas in the earthquake domain. The differences turn on the kinds of committees that hear testimony by dint of their formal jurisdiction or because they have a claim to or a stake in a set of issues.

Public works committees have historically been constituent-oriented and project-oriented bodies that seek to serve members' local political goals (Davidson and Oleszek 1994; Ripley and Franklin 1984; Smith and Deering 1984). This policy-making environment is characterized by mutual accommodation, logrolling, locally inspired projects, and close-knit, distributive policy relationships between the bureaucracy (in this case, the Army Corps of Engineers as the agency responsible for flood control and beach preservation projects) and the committee. In such an environment it is unlikely that a policy entrepreneur, either from inside or outside the committee, would be able to substantially change the way this business is transacted.

Reinforcing this policy making is the Army Corps of Engineers' project-oriented culture that is driven by the belief that engineered solutions are often the best ways to mitigate flood, storm surge, and erosion damage from hurricanes. Dams, flood-control projects, storm gates, breakwaters, and groins are also broadly popular in the local community, because of their perceived efficacy, because they protect local beaches against routine beach erosion (while sometimes causing sand losses elsewhere), and because of the economic benefits of large construction projects, regardless of their actual efficacy in protecting from normal erosion, flooding, or more serious damage by hurricanes. There are more effective ways of protecting lives and property—such as strictly limiting development on barrier islands or low-lying coastal areas—but these solutions, and the few people who propose them before committees, are likely to be in direct conflict with local development goals. Tourism and fishing, for example, are directly dependent on a seaside location and cannot readily be moved to safer areas; many people enjoy seaside living and are willing to assume the relatively small risk of a catastrophic hurricane striking their particular region of the coast.

We know that in disaster policy generally, scientific and technical information in the postevent phase is usually unimportant in decision making on disaster relief and reconstruction. In the wake of a hurricane (or even before one, as the data suggest) members of the public works committees are probably not particularly interested in broad scientific or technical discussions of the hurricane hazard and how to mitigate it. There are several reasons for this. First, such knowledge, particularly after events, does not help to advance member goals, which run more toward bringing home projects or ensuring the flow of disaster aid. Second, scientific knowledge of the major elements of the hazard—location and building practices—is already largely settled. Third, the application of such knowledge would often be in conflict with local land-use practices and economic development preferences. This makes for a less than fertile arena for policy entrepreneurs.

The earthquake domain is considerably different. The top two committees in this domain are more science-oriented than key committees in the hurricane domain. While there is a considerable constituency service element that motivates members of committees that deal in science, more policy-oriented members have joined the committees in recent years. Such members express interests in science and technology that go beyond individual district interests and encompass broader national policy issues (Smith and Deering 1984). Policy-oriented members are more likely to solicit expert opinion to better understand recent advances in earthquake science and engineering, and are more likely to promote programs that put this new knowledge into practice. This willingness to seek out and consider information may also be a function of the relatively low level of knowledge of earthquake dynamics compared to parallel knowledge in the hurricane domain.

In summary, the committees that take the greatest interest in hurricanes are constituency service committees that are most concerned with delivering federal largesse to members' districts under a relatively closed system of distributive policy making. In the earthquake domain, there is a more open type of policy making that is characterized by a desire to seek out and apply knowledge gained in disasters to mitigate future harms. If this characterization is true, it should be possible to identify policy entrepreneurs in Congress who work to advance programs to gather, analyze, and broadly disseminate scientific information on earthquakes. Fewer such policy entrepreneurs should be evident in the hurricane domain.

This characterization is clearly true. Beginning with the National Academy of Science's extensive multivolume reports on the 1964 Alaska earthquake, there has been an effort by the scientific community, supported by the federal government, to gather and disseminate technical information. The Earthquake Engineering Research Institute (EERI), a professional organization composed of scientists, engineers, social scientists, and others, has served as the center of a great deal of this professional activity. In addition, Senator Cranston of California was an important proponent of national policy making on earthquakes, having sponsored the most bills (seven) of any member of either the House or Senate in the period of this study. Cranston was key to the passage of the National Earthquake Hazards Reduction Act (NEHRA). There are few comparable efforts in the hurricane domain in any sense; there is no national hurricane program comparable to the NEHRA, there is no hurricane-related group as well organized as the EERI, there is no *coordinated* federal program to study the hazard[6], and there is little or no expressed demand, as the hearing record shows, from Congress to do so. These differences are reflected in Congress's drawing on far fewer expert witnesses to discuss hurricanes than are heard in the earthquake domain. This closed system results in few experts mobilizing to explain events or scientific issues or to press for policy change.

Groups and Policy Entrepreneurs in the Policy Community

The earthquake domain is clearly dominated by scientific and technical experts, whereas officials of the legislative and executive branch, whose concerns run mostly toward disaster relief, are more important in the hurricane domain. The only scientific groups represented in the hurricane domain are those charged with weather forecasting. If we very broadly define the scientific community to encompass the Weather Service and the Corps of Engineers (the public and civil works categories), the scientific community contributes a bare 8.5 percent of testimony delivered in the hurricane policy community. Scientific testimony in the earthquake community accounts for 35 percent of the testimony in the domain; there is roughly four times more scientific activity in the earthquake community than in the hurricane community. This reflects the greater attention paid to scientific and technical issues in the earthquake domain, as well as the greater degree of mobilization and organization of the scientists who deal with this type of disaster.

The importance of scientific and technical expertise in the earthquake community, and the paucity of such input in the hurricane community, is further illustrated by the types of policy entrepreneurs who appear before congressional committees. My definition of a policy entrepreneur—in this case, a witness who testified more than twice—is a broad one and may be overinclusive. Representatives of the Federal Emergency Management Agency (FEMA), for example, may appear before committees to report on agency performance rather than to press for new policy. However, even with this potentially overbroad definition of a policy entrepreneur, there are very few witnesses who can fairly be called policy entrepreneurs in the hurricane community. Of the individuals identified as hurricane policy entrepreneurs, only the representatives of the National Hurricane Center have consistently provided scientific information to committees and, more importantly, have consistently related their knowledge to ways in which hazards could be reduced. Such testimony (10 out of 567, or 1.76 percent of all witnesses heard) constitutes a very small portion of the information presented in these hearings.

In the earthquake domain there are several identifiable policy entrepreneurs, the vast majority of which represent scientific and technical interests or organizations. Of the thirteen earthquake policy entrepreneurs identified, all but two have some scientific or technical affiliation. Of the nonscientists, as discussed previously, Senator Cranston was a crucial policy entrepreneur in this domain and an important supporter of the 1977 National Earthquake Hazards Reduction Act.

Combining knowledge of who participates, where they participate, and what they say completes the picture of these policy communities.

There is clearly a more active professional community in the earthquake domain than in the hurricane domain. The earthquake community is composed of more active policy entrepreneurs who keep issues of seismic safety and hazard mitigation on the agenda, to some extent, even without a particular high-status event. Still both the earthquake and hurricane communities are quite sensitive to events, and when such an event is high on the agenda, disaster relief is the highest item on the agenda.

An Example: Earthquake Policy Entrepreneurship

The persistent theme underlying the story in this chapter is the importance of an active core policy community and policy entrepreneurs to advance issues on the agenda. This is entirely consistent with Paul Sabatier's (1988) theories of policy entrepreneurship as an important element of policy debate and change and John Kingdon's (1995) analysis of the role of policy entrepreneurs in joining problem and solution elements to make new policy. The existence of such entrepreneurs was crucial for the enactment of the National Earthquake Hazards Reduction Act of 1977 (NEHRA). The absence of such a community in the hurricane domain has meant a corresponding lack of such a program to deal with damaging hurricanes.[7] A brief review of the legislative history of the NEHRA shows how a combination of policy entrepreneurship, propitious circumstances, and, as Kingdon says, "an idea whose time has come" combined to result in active policy making and law making. The trigger, however, of policy making was at least one crucial focusing event.

In the theory of focusing events, the occurrence of a relatively large event should lead to noticeable increases in agenda activity. Yet, the mere fact of an event is not enough to lead to longer term agenda attention and policy change. The problem revealed by the focusing event needs to find an advocate who will continue to press the issue on the agenda even after the immediate attention to the problem has diminished. As mentioned earlier, a key earthquake policy entrepreneur was Senator Cranston of California. His interest in the earthquake problem was entirely sensible, as Senator Cranston represented a state with the largest number of people and value of property exposed to the earthquake hazard.

The San Fernando earthquake of 1971 was the event that moved Senator Cranston to action (Wehr 1977, 1412). After this event Senator Cranston introduced more legislation on earthquake relief and research programs than any other member of either house of Congress. Some of the legislation introduced by Senator Cranston and his colleagues was the sort of event-specific legislation that is common after disasters. For example, the Disaster Relief Act of 1970 allowed for the use of federal funds to repair public health care facilities. The 1971 earthquake did extensive damage to public and private health care facilities throughout the San Fernando valley (including the dramatic destruction of a good portion of the Veterans Administration Hospital in Sylmar) and dramatized the need for repairs to public and private health care facilities after a natural disaster. Representatives of private and charitable groups appealed to Congress for this aid provision, which was rather swiftly passed in the 1972 amendments to the Disaster Relief Act. These amendments allowed federal aid to private health care facilities damaged by natural disasters after January 1, 1971. Senator Cranston also used the event as an opportunity to advance a broader program of hazard reduction and earthquake prediction.

The scientific community was then engaged in the debate over increased research and hazard-reduction programs for two reasons. Earthquake research and prediction programs raised important scientific and social issues that natural scientists and social scientists were called upon to analyze and explain. In addition, the academic and scientific communities mobilized in support of earthquake research, both on good policy grounds and to increase the funding, visibility, and prestige afforded their ongoing research projects.

In spite of the magnitude of the San Fernando earthquake and the flurry of postdisaster attention, the 1971 earthquake was insufficient to move earthquakes to a high priority on the federal decision agenda. Senator Cranston's bills languished in the Senate, rarely reaching the floor. When in 1976 a package of legislation that foreshadowed the NEHRA passed the Senate, it failed to pass the House, having been left behind in the rush to adjourn.

But 1976 also saw the convergence of various elements that eventually contributed to the passage of the National Earthquake Hazards Reduction Act. First, a series of particularly damaging earthquakes in China, Italy, and Guatemala killed well over 600,000 people, illustrating how dangerous and costly truly large earthquakes can be. While these events were unlikely by themselves to move Congress to action— foreign events tend to be less important in domestic policy making (Smith 1992)—these events did reinforce the sense, triggered by the San Fernando earthquake, that the threat from earthquakes is serious. Second, the scientific community was abuzz over purported successes in earthquake prediction in China (which turned out to be overstated) and over a 100-mile-long uplift along the San Andreas fault, known as the "Palmdale Bulge," that many scientists felt could be a sign of increasing strain on the fault and, therefore, an impending earthquake.

These elements led to increasing concern in members of Congress from earthquake-prone areas. Finally, two prominent scientists were raising the earthquake issue on the scientific and congressional agendas. President Ford's science advisor, H. Guyford Stever, filed the Newmark Report (named for its principal investigator), "that said the time was right for a massive infusion of funds to improve prediction capabilities and minimize quake damage" (Wehr 1977, 1412). As CQ noted, President Carter's science advisor was Frank Press, "geophysicist and prominent advocate of earthquake forecasting," who energetically advanced the cause of earthquake research and hazard reduction in the executive branch.

John Kingdon argues that the search for the genesis of any policy is likely to result in "infinite regress." The best we can do is to identify critical moments in the history of policies that seem to have turned the tide in favor of new policies or ideas. One such critical moment in the earthquake domain is the San Fernando earthquake; no such critical moment seems to have emerged in the hurricane domain during the period of this study, although the establishment by FEMA of an in-house hurricane program after Hurricane Andrew suggests that Andrew may become the hurricane domain's critical moment. However, the long-run influence of Andrew on public policy is not yet clear. While all the other elements of the earthquake story were important, it seems fair to say that the San Fernando earthquake was the major impetus for change and that Senator Cranston was a primary agent of change. This event raised elite sensitivity to the earthquake hazard, so that later events and scientific discoveries resonated much more strongly among those who were concerned with the hazard, as well as with those who were just beginning to realize that the threat was important.

This history also shows a limitation of the focusing event as a determinant of agenda change. Clearly, the empirical research and this history shows that the San Fernando earthquake was an important event, but it was insufficient to result in broad policy change immediately. Rather, this history shows that focusing events are important to agenda change, but that other factors are needed to translate agenda activity into new or improved policy.

CONCLUSIONS: IMPLICATIONS FOR THE THEORY OF FOCUSING EVENTS

The empirical models presented in this chapter provide general support for the hypotheses introduced in chapter 2. Clearly, natural disasters serve as focusing events, influencing the news and congressional agendas. The relative importance of the event attributes in the models varies between the domains, however, and these differences reveal important differences between the two types of natural disasters.

The earthquake domain reflects an internal mobilization style of agenda setting in which issues are promoted on the congressional agenda by a few policy entrepreneurs. These advocates normally must wait for an opportunity—usually a disaster—to advance disaster policy on the congressional agenda and to generate public support for the new policy (Cobb, Ross, and Ross 1976). In contrast to members of traditional policy monopolies, many of these experts in the disaster domains would welcome more open politics and policy making, particularly in the preevent period, if for no other reason than to induce the public to participate in planning for the protection of their lives and property. Where low-probability risks are diffuse and attention is low, focusing events may draw attention to issues and induce, if not participation, greater public attention to a problem. It is therefore the disaster itself—not the activities of interest groups or even of professionals and policy entrepreneurs—that triggers greater agenda activity. But, as is evident in the analysis of the hurricane community in this chapter, the absence of an active core group of scientific and technical professionals makes it particularly difficult to elevate disaster prevention on that agenda (May 1985, 195). While many disaster policies were made in the wake of large disasters, the types of policies made—largely focusing on relief rather than on mitigation or prevention—reflect the bifurcation of disaster policy making into two concerns: mitigation, on the one hand, and relief on the other. Postevent politics, when disaster policy is most salient, centers on relief measures rather than mitigation.

When local representatives and victims hold and attend hearings on disasters, their comments are likely to be critical of disaster-relief policy, but are quite unlikely to deal meaningfully with existing or prospective mitigation policy. May found that "typically, [disaster] hearings consisted of various local officials' berating governmental relief efforts for the disaster that was being investigated, along with demands for new relief provisions as part of the general disaster relief act" (May 1985, 26). This is clearly reflected in the earthquake and hurricane hearings reviewed in this study. In the immediate aftermath of large disasters, there is a great deal more negative commentary from citizens and local government officials than there is between events, where disaster policy is as a "policy without a public" and interest is low.

The sudden increase in attention on immediate, postevent relief issues means that the policies that elected officials (acting on behalf of or in concert with a public mobilized temporarily and in response to a particular event) advocate in response to an event may not be congruent with what the active, professional members of the community consider to be the most important issues. The normative question of whether this results in good or bad policy will not be taken up here. The implication for policy makers is that there is a need to channel highly transient public energy and interest in the disaster threat not just to rebuilding the community, but to reconstructing policy so that the next disaster, wherever it occurs, can be more effectively mitigated, thereby reducing disaster-relief costs and suffering.

The stark difference between the earthquake and hurricane domains suggests at least two conclusions. First, while the theory is generally supported, one cannot suppose that what might appear to be similar types of events will have parallel effects on the agenda. No two policy domains within the broader rubric of "natural disasters" are precisely alike. In just this study, hurricanes and earthquakes differ in the geographical areas in which disasters are most likely to occur, the frequency and periodicity of the disasters, and, most important, the nature of the policy communities themselves. Thus, while the theory is generally supported and may very well apply broadly to other types of natural disasters, the relative importance of the event attributes may differ considerably among the different types of disasters.

Second, the modeling results reveal differences in the mobilization of political entrepreneurs, policy makers, experts, and ordinary citizens. This is a key finding that was not expected at the outset of the study, and which was not initially considered in the theory. The conclusions of this finding are twofold. First, an analysis of focusing events can reveal important differences between policy domains that may not be entirely evident at first glance. These differences may illuminate issues from which policy makers could learn that, while natural disasters are often unfortunate and tragic, they provide opportunities to alert citizens and elected officials to these threats and may provide an impetus for more effective policy making. For example, a determination that rarity is more important than deaths or property damage seems to reveal that it is the novelty of the event, rather than the human and economic toll, that gains the greatest attention. Knowing this might induce real or potential members of the policy domain to focus more on damage mitigation than on simply responding to the rare event.

Furthermore, the nature and composition of a policy community before or without an event will have a considerable influence on the nature of the postevent response. In particular, a domain in which a professional establishment exists is likely to see events trigger activity by professionals. These professionals can use the focusing event as an opportunity to create and explain policy positions and proposals. Such activity is predicated on the existence of such a community of professionals. In the example of policy entrepreneurship, the earthquake domain is characterized by an important policy entrepreneur in the legislative branch (Cranston), prominent supporters in the executive branch (Sever and Press), and an existing scientific, technical, and academic community that can be called upon to explain the problem and press for solutions.

Kingdon calls the combination of these critical elements "the fertile soil" in which policy ideas can take root and move up the agenda. Such an environment for policy making does not exist in the hurricane domain. Until it does, there is little prospect for the passage of comprehensive hurricane damage-reduction programs on the federal level on the same scale as the National Earthquake Hazards Reduction Act. This has significant implications for policy making in the hurricane community and may suggest a strategy whereby the crucial issues in the hurricane community could be better addressed. This very small and incoherent community may conclude from my analysis that it is important to create the sort of establishment Stallings (1995) described in the earthquake domain. This "hurricane policy establishment" could provide policy makers who only occasionally visit this issue with sound analysis and consistent messages on what steps should be taken to mitigate the damage wreaked by future storms. Until such a community is formed, it seems clear that hurricane policy will continue to focus on disaster relief; while large hurricanes may trigger more testimony, that testimony will simply continue and intensify the prior debate over the nature and purpose of disaster relief.

4

Oil Spills as Focusing Events

On March 27, 1989, the supertanker *Exxon Valdez* ran aground on Bligh Reef, in Prince William Sound, Alaska, spilling 11 million gallons of North Slope crude oil into the waters of the sound and south-central Alaska. Almost immediately the news media converged on the site of the spill, beaming pictures of oiled shorelines, birds, and sea otters to a shocked and angry public.[1] While this shock was sincere, many people—environmentalists, fishers, and elected officials—suggested that this spill was no fluke. Rather, they argued, such a spill was an inevitable result of the nation's dependence on fossil fuels and of federal and state decisions to exploit Alaska's oil wealth (Bookchin 1989).

A particularly important outcome of this oil spill was the enactment of the federal Oil Pollution Act of 1990. This legislation, enacted eighteen months after the *Exxon Valdez* spill, ended a nearly 14-year-long deadlock over how to streamline and strengthen federal oil pollution laws. The story of the *Exxon Valdez* oil spill and the passage of the Oil Pollution Act is a particularly apt example of focusing events and agenda change. In this case, it seems more than coincidental that significant legislation on oil spills passed so rapidly after the spill, whereas before the *Exxon Valdez* the passage of such legislation was at an impasse. The *Exxon Valdez* spill was the key event that finally broke the deadlock, gave policy makers a new sense of urgency, and ultimately resulted in legislation.

In this chapter I explain how oil spills serve as focusing events. While the *Exxon Valdez* spill was both spectacular and a key turning point in the history of federal oil spill policy, there have been other oil spills. Most spills are relatively small—less than 1,000 gallons—and attract relatively little attention. But truly large oil spills, such as the Santa Barbara oil well blowout in 1969 and the grounding of the *Argo Merchant* off Nantucket in 1976, gain considerable attention. These spills conjured vivid and enduring images of environmental and aesthetic damage, and they resulted in increased public and congressional attention to the problems of oil spills. In this chapter I assess whether the *Exxon Valdez* spill was a fluke in agenda or legislative terms, and whether other spills have had a similar influence on the agenda.

OIL SPILL POLICY CONTEXT:
THE ENVIRONMENTAL MOVEMENT

Much as earthquake or hurricane policy can be located in a broader context of natural disaster policy, oil spills are contained in the politics of environmental policy. As will be shown in this section, some form of environmental politics has been important in American national policy making for over 100 years. Yet, the most important political advances in environmentalism and its most important policy outcomes came in the 1960s. The increase in interest in the environment and the increase in public concern about oil spills were not coincidental. Rather, greater public interest in the quality of the environment made oil spills more dramatic and salient than they had been just a few years before.

Cochran, Mayer, Carr and Cayer (1986), Dunlap and Mertig (1992), and Cable and Cable (1995, 54–55) argue that the environmental movement was born in the late 1800s, when American territorial expansion slowed and human effects on natural resources became more apparent. In this era Yellowstone National Park and the national forest system were created, and John Muir formed the Sierra Club, the oldest of the major environmental groups, in 1892. This era was characterized by a conservationist style of resource management that continued through the 1930s. The New Deal stressed programs to promote soil conservation, improvements to national parks and other lands through the Civilian Conservation Corps, and the like. During the World Wars, however, the war effort moved conservationism off the nation's agenda. Millions of gallons of oil were spilled in American coastal waters during World War II, when tankers were sunk by German submarines in the Atlantic Ocean and the Gulf of Mexico. Clearly, such environmental degradation was unlikely to raise much concern in the midst of an all-out war, and the "situation" of oil spills, which were a consequence of war, did not achieve problem status, particularly considering more pressing issues.

Nor was environmentalism an important feature of the American political and social agenda after World War II. The major goals of American policy in this period were economic growth and national security. Environmental consciousness was not a major feature of American life until the publication of Rachel Carson's book *Silent Spring* (1962), which outlined the dangers of chemical pollution, particularly highly toxic pesticides such as DDT, and alerted Americans to the possibility of long-term, irreversible environmental damage.

The late 19th century and the New Deal era are considered to be the first and second waves of the environmental movement, although the concern in these periods was mostly resource conservation rather than more comprehensive concern with the environment as an interrelated system worthy of protection in its own right. *Silent Spring* marked the beginning of a third wave of concern with the environment. Carson's book, and other analyses that followed, showed how environmental problems were not simply an issue of scarce resources that needed to be carefully husbanded. Instead they were the product of complex social, economic, and technological factors that could lead to greater environmental damage than had ever occurred in human history (Dunlap and Mertig 1992, 2).

While *Silent Spring* was undoubtedly important in defining the environmental issue, it was just one of three related factors that, taken together, signaled a new era of environmental consciousness. *Silent Spring* was akin to a change in the indicators of a problem (Kingdon 1995), not a dramatic event that can lead to "alarmed discovery" of a problem (Downs 1972). Such changes in indicators are likely to resonate primarily with people who are most interested in or affected by a problem area.

The second factor was the changes in social trends that came together to provide a propitious era for increasing public consciousness of—and group mobilization because of—environmental degradation. Before this third wave of environmentalism, "many other earlier warning signs" of environmental decay "did not stir such a strong reaction." These changes included the transition to a postindustrial economy and public dissatisfaction with broad areas of public policy and government action generally, such as race relations and the Vietnam War (Cochran et al. 1986, 107). The late 1960s and early 1970s were watershed years in American politics and life, and the environmental movement is one enduring result of this turmoil.

A third factor was a series of dramatic environmental catastrophes, including the burning of the Cuyahoga River in 1968, the deaths of 80 people due to air pollution-related ailments in New York City in 1966, and the Santa Barbara oil spill of 1969 (Cable and Cable 1995). The Santa Barbara spill galvanized the public, interest groups, politicians, and the news media to action. This spill provided dramatic visual images of environmental catastrophe and was an event that could be constructed as a battle of good (the people of Santa Barbara) versus evil (oil companies and, to some extent, government) (Easton 1972). In the wake of this spill and other events and legislative activity, environmentalism remained as a potent social movement throughout the seventies, contradicting Downs' assertion that interest in the environment would substantially diminish as people realized the costs of environmental protection (Mitchell, Mertig, and Dunlap 1992, 15).

The environmental movement (as opposed to the conservation movement) is a relatively new force in American politics. Oil spills did not create this movement but, once this movement began to stir, focusing events such as oil spills became much more important. The Santa Barbara oil spill, the first major spill in the fifty states in the period of this study, occurred at the right time to mobilize the public, media, and elected officials. Had the spill occurred in 1949 or 1959, the reaction may have been much less alarmed and angry.

Group Dynamics in Environmental Politics

Unlike natural disaster politics, the environmental movement is characterized by high degrees of group political activity and conflict. The environmental policy community can be divided into three parts. First is the environmental movement and the interest groups that promote it. These groups vary considerably in their tactics and political styles. Older environmental groups, such as the Sierra Club and the Audubon Society, began as membership groups that led wilderness or nature outings and incidentally became involved in political activity to promote environmental protection. Sporting groups, such as the Izaak Walton League or Ducks Unlimited, support policies to promote the recreational value of the land. Groups such as the Environmental Defense Fund and the Natural Resources Defense Council (NRDC) were formed to lobby and to litigate on behalf of environmental protection. Groups such as Earth First! and Greenpeace concentrate more on direct action, such as blockading whaling ships or protesting near environmentally damaging industries (Mitchell, Mertig, and Dunlap 1992).

The second part of the policy community encompasses government actors at the national, state, and local level. While this study considers federal policy making, all these levels are represented before congressional committees. It is impossible, however, to attribute unity of interests to these actors, particularly at the state or federal level. At the national level, the Environmental Protection Administration (EPA) is often in conflict with the Minerals Management Service (MMS), the arm of the Interior Department that administers the offshore oil leasing program. Environmental goals often conflict with national economic goals, and thus engender differences in priorities within government. Such conflicts are apparent at the state level as well. The state of Alaska, whose Department of Environmental Conservation is charged with approving contingency plans for oil spills, derives well over 80 percent of its revenues from the oil industry. Alaskan agencies, like the federal and other state governments, therefore must balance their allegiances to economic growth and business development against environmental needs, and thus have conflicting goals and agendas.

The third broad category in the environmental policy community is the private sector. In this study, the oil industry and its affiliates are considered in this category. Such affiliates include shipbuilders, tank and barge operators and owners, insurance companies, terminal operators, and pipeline operators. The private sector's interests are clearly in reducing the costs of doing business while maintaining access to oil for extraction, shipment, refining, and marketing. Still, this group is not monolithic. While requirements for double-hull tankers had long been resisted by the oil companies, shipbuilders welcomed the double-hull requirements of the Oil Pollution Act of 1990. The act would increase work for shipbuilders, who would build new tankers or retrofit old ones.

These three types of actors can be categorized into overarching advocacy coalitions. Advocacy coalitions are clusters of interest groups that coalesce based on certain key group values to advance their policy goals. In the environmental policy domain, the values that come into play include economic growth, free enterprise, economic or social justice, and environmental protection. There are two main advocacy coalitions in the oil spill domain. One coalition, dominated by environmental interests, consists of groups that support tighter regulation of the oil industry in the interest of environmental protection. The other, an industry-led coalition, argues that further environmental measures are unnecessary (because the claimed harms are not real), would damage the nation's economic health, or would cost more than the value derived from environmental protection. Government agencies tend to split between these two positions, with agencies charged with promoting resource use, such as the Mineral Management Service, arrayed against agencies that are charged with making or enforcing environmental law, such as the Coast Guard or the EPA. Given the redistributive, public, and conflictual nature of these disputes, and the conflicting pressures on government to address both economic and environmental interests, environmental policy making is high on the federal government's agenda. Congressional leaders, members of the cabinet, and the president himself are called upon to make policy and settle disputes between conflicting interests inside and outside the government.

Trade-offs and Compromise in Environmental Policy

Conflicts over environmental policy are inevitable because of the very nature of the issues being discussed. First, the issues involve core beliefs that conflict: free enterprise versus government regulation of business, or the preservation of resources versus the belief in the need, desirability, or even the religious obligation to exploit those resources. Coalescence on and conflict over core beliefs is a defining characteristic of advocacy coalitions. Second, conflict is likely to occur because, over time, a very rough balance of resources exists to press a particular advocacy coalition's claims. In the oil case, oil companies can spend millions of dollars on public relations campaigns, lobbyists, and lawyers. Most analysts, particularly those whose sympathies lie with the environmental cause, would suggest that this is a permanent imbalance and advantage in favor of oil companies. For example, Molotch argues:

> What the citizens of Santa Barbara learned through their experience was that the parties competing to shape decision-making on oil in Santa Barbara do not have equal access to the means of 'mobilizing bias.' The Oil/ Government combine had, from the start, an extraordinary number of advantages. Lacking ready access to media, the ability to stage events at will, and a well-integrated system of arrangements for achieving their goals (at least in comparison to their adversaries), Santa Barbara's citizens have met with repeated frustrations (Molotch 1970, 102).

As Molotch notes, some of the mainstream routes to political access tend to be exercises in which local residents can let off steam, to little effect. Other means of political expression, such as direct action or protests, tend to be dismissed as outside the mainstream. This stands in contrast to my findings in the natural disaster domain. In hearings after earthquakes and hurricanes, I found that field hearings provide an opportunity for victims to vent their frustration. Field hearings are also very important in gaining the attention of elected officials, who wish to be seen as sympathetic to victims, and the bureaucracy, which also wishes to be seen as sympathetic while trying to minimize criticism or interference from elected officials.

I find that the political situation is not as bleak as Molotch argues in the wake of focusing events, particularly large environmental disasters. Molotch's argument is to a large extent predicated on the dynamics of a "pseudoevent," or an event that can be stage-managed by an interest that has a stake in glossing over a disaster. However, it is often nearly impossible to conceal a disaster such as a huge oil spill (or even a serious nuclear power plant accident, which is conceivably easier to conceal from the public for a while, as I discuss in the next chapter). In such cases, environmental organizations gain a resource edge through important environmental disasters, such as oil spills, which in turn lead to the mobilization of existing members and the enlistment of new members to the environmental cause, and, for a short time, the mobilization of bias that results in legislation. These members are mobilized to press their elected officials for more stringent environmental regulation. Such legislation may not go as far as environmental groups would prefer, but is likely to represent an improvement over the status quo before the event. A permanent tug of war thus results, with neither side of the debate able to claim total victory.

The third reason for political conflict is the nature of the American political system and the unlikelihood of sweeping change. The constitutional system of checks and balances prizes deliberate action, compromise, and incrementalism over rapid, comprehensive change (Rosenbaum 1991). Every change in environmental policy, whether an advance or a retreat, is likely to face substantial opposition that may exploit structural features of American political institutions to delay policy making. Group conflict, and a considerable amount of stasis, is a continuing feature of environmental politics. Policy change is therefore more likely to occur due to an exogenous shock to the political system and the policy domain than through concerted group action by itself (Baumgartner and Jones 1993). Focusing events provide such a shock to the system.

FEDERAL OIL SPILL POLICY, 1960 TO 1990

The state of federal oil spill policy in the past thirty-five years can be summarized by using three themes: the disjointedness of federal policy dealing with oil spills, the history of attempts to join oil spill liability and cleanup schemes with hazardous materials liability and cleanup into one "super" bill, and the problem of federalism versus federal preemption of state law. I do not consider international conventions that deal with oil spills, in large part because the United States, fearing threats to states' rights and national sovereignty, has declined to ratify these conventions (Gallagher 1990).

Before 1970 there was no legal regime to make oil spillers liable for cleanup costs and damages resulting from oil spills. The only tool available to make claims against shipping was the Limitation of Liability Act of 1851, which governed tort law related to shipping. As late as 1979 Mendelsohn and Fidell could state that "so far as concerns vessel owner liability for oil pollution damage . . . , the principal governing law in the United States today is, with some exceptions, one that was adopted almost 130 years ago" (Mendelsohn and Fidell 1979, 476). As applied by the courts, this statute often resulted in absurdly low liability limits, so "ways have been tried—and found—to 'break the limits,'" mainly by "showing that the damage was done or incurred with 'the privity or knowledge of' the owner—in which event the owner's liability becomes unlimited" (Jones 1989, 10335). The complexity of this statute and the various devices which plaintiffs and defendants can use to increase or decrease liability make this law unsuitable for pressing spillers to clean up oil. Nor does this law cover spills from offshore oil activities.

The inadequacies of the Limitation of Liability Act and a growing concern with the environmental damage done by oil spills led to the enactment of Section 311 of the Federal Water Pollution Control Act Amendments of 1972, popularly known as the Clean Water Act. This legislation "declared that as a national policy, there should be no discharges of oil into the navigable waters of the United States, the adjoining shorelines, or from vessels operating in the contiguous zones" (Jones 1989, 10333). In pursuit of these goals, the law established liabilities for owners of oil facilities and for shipowners, at $8 million for fixed facilities and the lesser of $100 per gross ton or $14 million for ships. Amendments in 1978 raised only shipowners' liability to $150 per gross ton for ships and $125 per ton for barges.

Section 311 also required that a national oil spill contingency plan be established, and for the first time mandated the creation of a revolving fund to cover costs incurred by the federal government in cleaning up oil spills. This fund (financed in large part by congressional appropriations, with the remainder coming from fines) never reached its authorized size of $35 million, reaching at most $24 million in 1985. "[A]s of June 1985 [the fund] had a balance of $7.3 million, little more than pocket change when faced with cleaning up a spill of the size of the *Exxon Valdez*," largely because assessed fines were not keeping up with cleanup costs (Jones 1989, 10334–35).

In 1973 the Trans-Alaska Pipeline Authorization Act (TAPAA) created a similar fund for cleanups related solely to the Trans-Alaska Pipeline System (TAPS). This fund differs from the Section 311 fund in that it was solely funded by a five cents per barrel tax on oil loaded onto ships at Port Valdez, not through taxpayer funds as in the 1970 law. The size of the TAPS fund was capped by law at $100 million. This level was reached in 1981, but investments raised its balance to $250 million. This fund was not called upon to clean up the *Exxon Valdez* oil spill, as Exxon chose to rely on its resources, but this fund is still smaller than the costs of cleaning up the *Exxon Valdez* spill.

Another enactment dealing with liability limits and funds was the Deepwater Port Act of 1974, which provided for a cleanup fund and a liability limit of $20 million for ships and $50 million for deepwater ports. Such ports are designed to unload supertankers far offshore, since their draft is often greater than can be accommodated in port. Oil is moved from offshore ports by pipeline to shoreside facilities. Only one such port has been established, in Louisiana.

By the mid-1970s, with the perceived need to exploit more of the nation's energy resources, offshore exploration became more urgent. In 1978 the Congress passed the Outer Continental Shelf Lands Act Amendments. "It established yet a third federal oil spill fund, this one with $200 million to cover spills from offshore production facilities and vessels transporting oil from these facilities. A $35 million liability limit for damages and *unlimited* liability for cleanup were imposed"

(Jones 1989, 10335, emphasis in original). Congress also passed the Tanker Safety Act of 1978 (P.L. 95-474), which addressed technical aspects of tanker equipment, personnel, and the like. However, this did not address the problems of cleanup and prevention of spills, and its passage did not represent the major step toward preventing oil spills that environmentalists and their allies had sought.

In summary, federal oil spill policy before the passage of the Oil Pollution Act was disjoint and duplicative, and yet was woefully inadequate to prevent or address a large oil spill. These laws did not have a uniform standard of liability or defenses, although the trend was toward limiting exclusions and defenses to the point where, in the Trans-Alaska Pipeline Authorization Act, an act of God was not, by itself, an adequate defense. Nor did these laws require direct federal action to respond to oil spills, which led to valuable time being lost as responsibility for cleanup was debated among the Coast Guard, the States, the shippers, insurers, and the owners of the oil being transported.

Two of these laws—the Trans-Alaska Pipeline Authorization Act of 1973 (TAPAA) and the Deepwater Port Act of 1974 (DWPA)—provided for a taxing and trust fund mechanism to defray the cost of oil spill cleanup, response, and compensation beyond certain liability limits. These laws were incremental policies intended to deal with oil spills in particular areas, such as Prince William Sound, and the Gulf of Mexico in the TAPAA and the OCS Lands Amendments. A comprehensive solution was not established, perhaps because, as noted earlier, incrementalist approaches are easier to achieve (Lindblom 1979; Lindblom 1959). It is also quite likely that any spill provisions were included in these laws as much to overcome opposition to the passage of the basic legislation as they were to provide a workable compensation, liability, and cleanup scheme.

Attempts to create a comprehensive federal oil spill liability, compensation, and response bill began in 1975, and intensified in 1976 in response to spills from a number of large oil tankers (Vaden 1977). In spite of these spills, Congress was unable for years to agree on a comprehensive solution to the problem of oil spills. Two factors in particular may have delayed the passage of such legislation.

The first of these barriers was the attempt by other interests to address other issues by using the oil spill issue as a way to gain agenda status. One of these attempts—an effort to establish a cargo preference scheme so that more oil would enter United States ports on U.S. flag ships—was rather quickly turned aside when oil industry officials failed to support it. Environmental groups also cited the rather poor loss record of U.S. flag ships compared to some other nations' fleets.

A far more important example of the oil spill issue being combined with other issues was the "major addition of a parallel regime for the cleanup of hazardous substances" (Jones 1989, 10335) to oil spill legislation. Legislation to address hazardous discharges was an important part of President Carter's and Senator Muskie's (D-Maine) legislative agendas, the urgency of which was enhanced by the Love Canal and Times Beach catastrophes. The effect was that "congressional attention was diverted from oil spills to hazardous wastes" (ibid.).

Senator Muskie attached hazardous waste provisions to S 2083, the Senate counterpart to House oil spill legislation (HR 6803) in 1978. The first attempt to address chemical spills was hampered by an unclear and incomplete funding mechanism and perceptions that the funding would fall unfairly on oil producers or producers of nonhazardous chemicals, neither of which wanted to be compelled to pay for the others' spills. In spite of this false start, by 1979 momentum had built to the point where oil spill legislation was subordinated to the passage of a chemical cleanup scheme, resulting in the Comprehensive Environmental Response, Compensation, and Liability Act of 1980, popularly known as the Superfund law. The addition of chemical spills and the waning memory of recent oil spills is a classic illustration of how quickly the window of opportunity to create new policy can close as new problems intrude on the agenda, or how the revelation of one problem can lead policy entrepreneurs to suggest that the solutions being considered can extend to similar problems (Kingdon 1995; Walker 1977).

Once the hazardous materials scheme was in place, it became clear that the passage of a comprehensive oil spill liability and compensation regime was not in the offing. From its inauguration until 1984, the Reagan administration refused to support any oil spill plan. The Senate and the House remained at loggerheads over whether state laws should be preempted by federal law and the extent to which the United States should conform to international standards in this field. The divisions between the House and Senate were summarized by Representative Walter Jones of the House Merchant Marine and Fisheries Committee. In his 1989 article in the *Environmental Law Reporter*, he noted that the committee had passed an oil spill bill in the 94th "and every subsequent Congress," while the Senate had not passed such a bill. "The primary stumbling block has been the inability to reach agreement on the preemption of state oil spill cleanup funds and state liability laws" (Jones 1989, 10333).

In general, senators (particularly those from coastal states) supported the states' rights to tax oil companies and carriers to fund cleanups, to compel cleanup action by spillers, and to set their own liability regimes that were sometimes more stringent than the federal system. Senators from coastal states were particularly insistent that there be no preemption and had the comfort of a favorable ruling of the Supreme Court. In *Askew* v. *American Waterways Operators, Inc.* (411 U.S. 325, 1973), the Court held that existing federal oil spill legislation did not preempt or preclude states from enacting their own spill cleanup and liability schemes.[2] State governments were unwilling to cede any of their power to the federal government in this area, and environmentalists also supported the preservation of states' powers to enact their own spill laws, since state environmental laws were often stricter and enforced more vigorously than federal law.

In general, members of the House of Representatives were much more inclined to preempt state law in favor of a uniform national law that would alleviate confusion and duplication, and which would be more closely harmonized with international standards. Preemption was also supported by some federal officials, who felt that a uniform national system of liability would be more predictable and therefore more effective than a patchwork of state regulations. The oil and shipping industries were particularly supportive of preemption, since they were exposed to liability from the federal government and one or more states—a spill in the Delaware River could conceivably expose the shipper to liability in Pennsylvania, New Jersey, and Delaware. Of course, there were two motivations for this position, with the oil companies and their contractors seeking to limit their exposure to liability, while federal officials (as well as some environmentalists) sought administrative coherence and efficiency (National Response Team 1989, 34). Some commentators sympathetic to the environmental movement were also concerned about the proliferation of state laws. They argued that this "web" of law and regulations led to confusion and inefficient application of the law against polluters (Davidson 1990, 59; Gallagher 1990). However, most environmentalists feared that preempting state law would result in lower federal liability limits for tanker operators.

The resolve of the Senate to hold fast on preemption was stiffened by the ascension of Senator George Mitchell (D-Maine) to the majority leadership. Senator Mitchell represented a coastal state with important interests in coastal and ocean resources (and no oil production); he made clear in 1986 that he would not support any legislation that preempted state law (*Congressional Record*, Sept. 27, 1986: S14143). The majority leader's persuasive powers on these matters were great, and the impasse stood at this point until 1989.

The *Exxon Valdez* spill was the event that tipped the balance in favor of more stringent oil spill legislation. "For many of the 15 years that Congress spent laboring in vain to produce a national oil-spill liability law, some frustrated backers predicted that it would take a catastrophic oil spill to break the legislative stalemate. In 1989 that catastrophe happened" (Congressional Quarterly 1989b, 682). The spill, and Exxon's response to the spill, caused so much public and congressional anger that it was a primary cause for the House's dropping its insistence on preemption. Perhaps the most spectacular outcome of the *Exxon Valdez* spill was this dramatic turnaround on the preemption issue. The House of Representatives went from offering limited solutions, in which states could tax oil activities and spend on cleanup but could not impose their own liability regimes, to a total adoption of the Senate position that no preemption would be permitted. As a sop to those supporting international liability and compensation systems, the final act did endorse U.S. participation in such oil spill conventions, but the law was passed with the full knowledge that its provisions did not conform with international liability regimes. With the preemption issue out of the way, oil spill legislation passed relatively easily, and President Bush signed the Oil Pollution Act of 1990 (OPA) into law on August 18, 1990.

The OPA provides for vastly tougher penalties and liability for spillers of oil, allocates more resources for dealing with spills, and places more responsibility on the executive branch to respond to oil spill incidents promptly. The creation of the spill cleanup fund in the OPA was also a major accomplishment. The fund not only consolidated three smaller funds that were financed differently and served different purposes; it also created a fund bigger than had ever been established. At $1 billion such a fund may not be sufficient to clean up the largest spill, but it still comes closer to the costs of cleaning up a spill of the magnitude of the *Exxon Valdez* than did any of the other funds, separately or together.

AGENDA DYNAMICS IN THE OIL SPILL DOMAIN

In the models that follow, individual oil spills are the units of analysis. The data set contains fifty-five large oil spills identified between 1968 and 1990. As noted in chapter 2, this list of spills is neither a random nor comprehensive sample. The data set considers all major spills in this period and includes any spill mentioned in any congressional hearing in the period under study. The dependent variables of interest are measures of news and institutional "agenda activity," and encompass the measures of institutional and media agenda change and density as defined in the previous chapters. These measures discount events that are simply correlated with agenda change, without actually resulting in agenda change.

The independent variables are similar to those introduced in the analysis of natural disasters, except that the primary measure of damage in this case is the volume of oil spilled, rather than deaths or property damage. The volume of spill is an imperfect measure of the "real" impact of an oil spill. The damage done by a spill is less a function of the amount of oil spilled and more a function of the type of oil spilled (refined products evaporate more rapidly than crude oil) and where the oil is spilled, since spills in rivers, sounds, bays, or the like are more injurious to the environment than spills in the open ocean (Devanney, Protopapa, and Klock 1989). The imperfection of this measure is, in focusing event terms, less serious than it might seem because the actual damage done is less important than the perception of damage from spills. Thus, while the volume of oil may be technically less important, it is still the most accessible indicator of the magnitude of an oil spill, and is therefore one of the symbols that will be most widely propagated.

Table 4-1 shows the correlates of news and congressional agenda activity. Contrary to expectations, the scope of the event (in this case, defined as the number of people living in the counties where oil was spilled or landed on shorelines) is negatively correlated with agenda activity. This, combined with the nonsignificant results of the scope variable in the regression models here and in the natural disaster models, suggests that scope is generally not an important variable in focus-

TABLE 4-1   Event Attribute Models

	Correlation Coefficients	
	News Agenda Activity	*Congressional Agenda Activity*
Gallons Spilled	0.425	0.401
Rarity	0.425	0.485
Scope	−0.230	−0.066
	Regression Results[a]	
Adjusted R^2	0.193	0.200
F	5.315	5.504
p	0.003	0.002
N	55	55

[a]Dependent variables are news and congressional agenda activity, respectively. Variables are transformed to meet the requirements of OLS regression. Variables are defined in the text and the appendix.

ing event politics as modeled here. The explanation for the relative unimportance of scope is quite simple; oil spills are environmental disasters that injure ecosystems, not a large population of people. Thus, while the area in which the *Exxon Valdez* spilled its oil is sparsely populated, the magnitude of its effects on the ecosystem was so great that it became a news story. This large event in a sparsely populated area results in a negative relationship between scope and news coverage.

The two remaining variables reveal a subtle difference between the news and congressional agendas. In the news agenda the amount of oil spilled is more important, while the rarity of the spill—the time that has passed since the last spill of equal or greater magnitude—is more strongly correlated with the level of congressional agenda activity. This suggests a difference in the nature of these two agendas. The congressional agenda appears to be driven by the exceptional event as such; its size is relatively less important. The news, on the other hand, has a much shorter attention span, so the sheer size of any oil spill determines the response, even if two large spills occur relatively close together in time. One should not make too much of these differences, however, as the differences in these coefficients are relatively small.

Overall, oil spill influence on the congressional agenda is muted compared to the natural disaster domains. This is shown in the lower R^2 values in the regression models (Tables 4-1 and 4-2) and by the extent to which policy making in the domain is ongoing, rather than

TABLE 4-2 Political Model of the Congressional Agenda

Standardized Regression Coefficients

	Congressional Agenda Activity
News Change	0.392**
News Density	0.534**
Mobilization	0.222*
Scope	0.052
Mean Tone	0.128
Adjusted R^2	0.318
F	6.031
p	0.000
N	55

*$p<.05$ **$p<.01$

TABLE 4-3 Testimony, Field Hearings, and Testimony Centered on Events

		Testimony Type		
Hearing Type		Centered on an Event	All Others	Total
Field	Mean tone[a]	−0.541	−0.256	−0.442
	N	222	117	339
	Modal Policy[b]	Spill Cleanup and Response	Tanker Safety	Oil Field Development
Washington	Mean tone	−0.391	−0.019	−0.128
	N	258	622	880
	Modal Policy	Spill Cleanup and Response	Liability, Compensation and Costs	Liability, Compensation and Costs
Total	Mean tone	−0.460	−0.057	−0.216
	N	480	739	1219
	Modal Policy	Spill Cleanup and Response	Liability, Compensation and Costs	Liability, Compensation and Costs

Notes:
For total analysis of variance on mean tone: $F_{3,1215} = 27.101$, $p = 0.000$
For distribution of hearing type and testimony type, Chi-squared with 1 df = 134.111, $p<0.000$
[a]Tone is a measure of attitudes toward existing policy, where +1 indicates general support for existing policy, −1 indicates opposition to existing policy, and 0 is neutral.
[b]Policy type is the predominant topic discussed by the witness in a congressional hearing, based on the review of testimony in each domain.

disaster-driven (Tables 4-3 and 4-4). The latter tables show that participation in policy making, either by all witnesses before congressional committees, or just that offered by decision makers and policy entrepreneurs, tends not to focus solely on events. Rather, oil spill policy treats this problem as an ongoing issue that is punctuated, but not driven, by events. Saying that this domain is not primarily event-driven does not in any way suggest that events are unimportant. Spills have important implications for issue containment and expansion, which reveal the importance of spills in political conflict in the domain. I now turn to a discussion of these effects.

OIL SPILLS, CONFLICT, AND GROUP MOBILIZATION

The analysis here is similar to the findings in chapter 3, but for a rather different reason. In the oil spill models, tone was less important in the

TABLE 4-4   Decision Maker and Policy Entrepreneur Activity

| Testimony: | Decision makers[a] | | Policy Entrepreneurs[b] | |
	Centered on Event	Not Centered	Centered	Not Centered
N of witnesses	153	251	157	326
Mean Tone[c]	−0.288	−0.163	−0.420	−0.012
t		−1.790		−5.120
p (one tailed)		0.037		0.000

[a]Decision makers are witnesses in a policy-making role in the federal legislative or executive branch.
[b]Policy entrepreneurs are witnesses who appeared two or more times in hearings in their respective fields.
[c]Tone is attitude toward current policy, where −1 indicates dissatisfaction with current policy, and +1 indicates satisfaction with policy.

regression model than was expected. Instead, group conflict, rather than attitudes toward policy, was a more important political aspect of this model. However, the differences in tone between testimony centered on events and testimony not centered on events, and delivered by policy entrepreneurs and decision makers, show that oil spills trigger more testimony with a negative tone. Thus, those policy entrepreneurs who are mobilized by oil spills—that is, group leaders—nearly always oppose existing policy toward oil spills. The event does not change attitudes, per se; rather, it simply makes leaders and decision makers—whose attitudes toward oil spill policy are already negative—more visible and active. For the reasons reviewed next, groups that oppose existing policy are much more likely to be mobilized by oil spills and to use them as symbols to press their case than are defenders of the status quo.

Issue Containment and Social Construction

E.E. Schattschneider (1960/1975) was among the first to recognize the centrality of issue expansion in agenda setting and political conflict. The expansion of an issue or a conflict beyond the immediately affected population is crucial to the success of interest groups who seek to highlight a problem, particularly when the group promoting change is historically disadvantaged in some way. Environmental groups' major disadvantage is that they have fewer monetary resources to pursue their policy goals before Congress than have representatives of oil interests.

In my theory of focusing events, the images of the event provide potent resources that can, at least for a while, overcome these resource inequities and provide out-groups improved access to the political process. In turn, the oil companies can be expected to attempt to contain the conflict resulting from the oil spill. Although it is impossible to contain the fact of the oil spill itself, the predominant pattern is for oil companies to argue that the spill is not as bad as claimed and that any proposals to further regulate shipping, drilling, or other activities are disproportionate to the immediate event. As part of this tactic, in their testimony oil companies refer to oil spills as an abstract problem rather than referring to particular events.

The process of socially constructing the event—or, as Deborah Stone (1989) defines it, the process of creating causal stories of an event—is an important part of the process of issue containment and expansion. In the story of the failure of oil companies to fully contain the issue in big oil spills, it seems clear that issue containment failed because the oil advocacy coalition failed to create a causal story as compelling as the story told by the environmental coalition. This is not to say that the environmental story will always prevail over the oil story, for a number of reasons. This does mean that, in the near term, the oil companies will have an exceedingly difficult time explaining the spill in terms that the most casual observers will accept.

In the wake of the Santa Barbara spill, Union Oil's public relations effort began soon after a call to the local newspaper revealed the beginning of the spill. The Coast Guard official on the scene was worried that Unocal's public relations efforts had lulled Santa Barbarans into a belief that the worst had passed, even though the well was not fully capped for several months after the beginning of the spill (Steinhart and Steinhart 1972, 61). In the *Argo Merchant* spill, policy makers were assured that spills of this sort were quite rare and that the damage was likely to be minimal (Devanney, Protopapa, and Klock 1989). That the spill happened in the open ocean may have contributed to the rapid dissipation of interest in the spill, even by residents of Nantucket, who reported that the spill had a minimal affect on their livelihood (Fricke and Maiolo 1978).

Union Oil's strategy of issue containment was doomed to fail because the images of the spill were so widely propagated. Still, Union Oil attempted a strategy of problem redefinition to discount the importance of the event. The president of Union Oil claimed that the spill was not really a disaster and that "Mother nature had let us down," thereby reducing the spill to a natural disaster over which there was no possibility of human control (Potter 1973). Stone notes that such a move is an attempt to keep an accident defined as something unavoidable or uncontrollable. Such incidents are then generally dismissed by the public as something about which nothing can or should be done, thereby reducing the "problem" to a "condition" over which nothing could be done.

Molotch also argues that Union sought to contain the spill through what he calls a "creeping event." A creeping event "occurs when something is actually taking place, but when the manifestations of the event are arranged to occur at an inconspicuously gradual and piecemeal pace, thus avoiding some of the consequences which would follow from the event if it were immediately perceived to be occurring. . . . A creeping event has the consequence of diffusing resistance by withholding what journalists call a 'time peg' on which to hang the story" (Molotch 1970, 97). In the Santa Barbara case, the reconfiguration of the spill from a sudden event to a creeping event was impossible. The gush of oil from Platform A was anything but gradual. Although the oil company did not alert the news media of the spill, word of the spill reached the local newspaper within 24 hours of the blowout. Even without that notification, the mass of oil washing ashore would have been impossible to explain as anything but the result of a major spill.

With the spill being well out in the open, little could be done to construct the issue as anything but a major accident with severe aesthetic, if not environmental, consequences. The public relations war was on, and it focused on ten elements of the story:

> Each group sought advantageous coverage of such issues as (1) the volume of oil covering the ocean and beaches, (2) the extent of long- and short-term ecological damage from oil, (3) the economic and social costs which additional drilling or production would entail, (4) the energy needs of industry, (5) the aesthetic damage caused by oil platforms to the ocean-island horizon, (6) the likelihood of future spills, (7) the economic subsidies received by oil companies, (8) the social and business links between oil companies and governmental officials, (9) the "impracticality" and "idealism" of conservationists, and (10) the "irrational hysteria" and "selfishness" of antioil Santa Barbarans (Molotch and Lester 1975, 238).

The battle was joined, the issue expanded to a greater extent than oil company partisans would have preferred, and the event became a critical turning point in the history of the oil industry and the environmental movement.

An equally heated public relations war was fought over the impact of the *Exxon Valdez* spill. This interpretation of the spill notwithstanding, Exxon and its allies immediately attempted to contain this issue. Conrad Smith (1991) found that both the oil industry and environmentalists engaged in an effort to portray the spill in a manner favorable to their policy preferences. Exxon's strategy was actually quite inept in the near term. The CEO of the Exxon Corporation failed to visit the spill or even mention it for three weeks. This appeared to be a calculated effort to contain the issue; by not visiting the spill site, the president of the company was signaling that the spill was not sufficiently worthy of concern at the highest levels of the firm. This tactic backfired and projected an image of indifference. Their efforts at fixing blame elsewhere enraged the targets of blame, such as the Coast Guard and the state of Alaska generally, and Dennis Kelso, the Alaska Commissioner of Environmental Conservation, in particular. Commissioner Kelso rarely missed an opportunity to castigate Exxon or the Alyeska Pipeline Service Company, although it was his department that was charged with approving Alyeska's oil spill contingency plans. Even when Exxon began to have some technical successes in the cleanup of the spill, their public relations effort lagged far behind, failing to tell their side of the story (Satchell and Carpenter 1989, 68–69).

Ultimately, issue containment was quite difficult in the Exxon case for three reasons. The first is that the mobilization effect of this spill was particularly powerful, as I discuss in the following section. The second reason is that the magnitude and symbols of the spill were nearly impossible to contain, particularly in light of continued assurances by federal agencies, the oil companies, and the Alyeska Pipeline Service Company that the pipeline and the tanker systems were safe, that a spill of *Exxon Valdez*'s magnitude was highly unlikely and that, should a spill occur, the equipment and technology were available to clean it up. These points were dramatically and effectively refuted by the grounding of the *Exxon Valdez*. The third reason is that the spill was nearly impossible to depict as anything but an accident that resulted from human negligence, not an "act of God," as Exxon claimed in an effort to "lay early groundwork for its legal defense strategy" (Satchell and Carpenter 1989, 68–69).

The lesson for oil companies and their allies may be that, since efforts to actively contain conflict over oil spills by active public relations campaigns or blame fixing have generally failed, the best strategy may be to avoid discussing specific spills unless absolutely necessary, in hopes that the event will quickly be forgotten. Such a strategy would serve to draw as little attention to specific spills as possible. To assess whether such a strategy has been adopted, I isolated the top fifteen and bottom fifteen group types that testify in hearings about oil spills, ranked in order of the proportion of their testimony that is offered in response to a particular event. Thus, the top fifteen group types are those groups that delivered the most testimony in response to a particular oil spill, and the bottom fifteen are those group types whose witnesses were most likely to testify without direct reference to a particular oil spill.

The groups that were least likely to testify in direct response to a particular event are dominated by private-sector interests with ties to the oil industry, such as shipping, insurance, chemical, and shipbuilding companies. Of the fifteen least likely to testify in response to a particular event, no one group gave more than 14 percent of its testimony in direct response to a particular oil spill. The mean tone of all the witnesses appearing for these groups is 0.586 for all testimony offered in these hearings.

On the other hand, the groups that were most likely to testify in response to an event were mostly connected with citizens' organizations, academic institutions, and with state and local governments that deal with the immediate aftereffects of oil spills. The mean tone of the witnesses appearing on behalf of these groups is –0.373. These figures suggest that oil spills do mobilize different types of witnesses to appear before Congress, suggest the basis for the imbalance in the postevent period between groups supporting change and those who favor stasis, and reflect the degree of polarization in this domain. As discussed in the following section, these differences reveal environmental group mobilization in response to focusing events, while the mobilization of oil company and allied interests is less likely since these groups' goals are to minimize conflict, controversy, exposure, and publicity, thereby containing conflict and pressure for change to the extent possible.

Group Mobilization after Oil Spills

Thus far two things have been shown to happen in the immediate aftermath of oil spills. First, a potent set of symbols is created, of oiled shorelines, incompetent captains, and corporate neglect and incompetence. Second, industry immediately seeks to contain conflict, knowing that the spill cannot be ignored but that dissenting voices, if not countered, could lead to undesirable new policy.

Unfortunately for the oil companies, the spill itself is merely one of their headaches, for oil spills are so emotional and contain so many powerful symbols and images that they often lead to the mobilization of highly motivated environmental and citizens' groups that work to oppose oil company interests. Such mobilization was most prominent in the Santa Barbara and *Exxon Valdez* spills.

In the Santa Barbara spill, congressional hearings mainly served as a safety valve for citizen complaints about the spill and about Unocal's behavior, but did not result in substantive policy designed to deal with the spill problem (Molotch 1970). Such hearings might have been effective in containing conflict, had they been sincere attempts to find solutions to the problem. Instead, given their unsatisfying result for many Santa Barbarans, a number of local residents founded a new group to deal with their long-standing concerns over the activities of the oil industry in Santa Barbara channel. The story of the formation of the major group to grow out of this spill is instructive:

> On January 30, 1969, the organization GOO! was born. The story has been told many times of how artist Bud Bottoms, long a foe of oil, exclaimed to his boss 'We've got to get oil out.' The boss was Marvin Stuart, a General Electric public relations man with the necessary ear for slogans. As the story goes, he cried out 'That's it! GOO! We'll call it GOO! for Get Oil Out.' With relish, Bottoms and Stuart made plans for a mass organization named GOO, enlisting the help of former state senator Alvin Weingand, who became GOO's leader. . . . They got plenty of publicity but, to their profound frustration, little else in the way of satisfaction. Other action groups were formed. Santa Barbara Citizens for Environmental Defense, SBCED, chose the legal route for its main thrust. Of all the things that the citizens of Santa Barbara did, it was GOO that captured the public's sympathy and imagination most completely. Perhaps it was only because of Stuart's genius in giving the organization its name, but probably it was more than that. Probably it was a genuine upswelling of grass roots sympathy (Steinhart and Steinhart 1972, 112–113).

GOO continued its activities well into the 1970s, opposing further oil development offshore, and was instrumental in keeping oil development under state control within three miles of the shore line. But GOO was not created from whole cloth. Discontent about big oil, development pressures, and actual and potential environmental damage had been building for some time in Santa Barbara. Much of this opposition was dismissed by oil interests as the complaints of a small collection of malcontents who did not understand or appreciate the need for or the benefit of oil extraction. The Santa Barbara oil spill changed this. GOO was not a radical fringe group—it was composed of a fairly representative cross section of the community, whose common interest was to oppose continued oil drilling in Santa Barbara channel. An important element of the antioil movement was the fairly moderate local newspaper, the Santa Barbara News-Press (Nash, Mann, and Olson 1972, 5–9). The lesson for the oil companies is that had the Santa Barbara spill never happened, the News Press' highly critical reporting would not have appeared, GOO would not have formed, and the sentiments expressed by this group could still be dismissed as the complaints of a fringe group.

The Exxon Valdez spill, by contrast, did not lead directly to the creation of any new groups. But it did mobilize and make more visible groups that traditionally feared oil development and oil tanker traffic in Alaska. Such groups opposed the Trans-Alaska pipeline from the outset, and "cited dangers of pollution from oil spills in Alaskan waters and in Washington's Puget Sound to which oil would be hauled" (Congressional Quarterly 1972, 564). These groups included Common Cause, the Consumer Federation of America, Cordova District Fisheries Union, Defenders of Wildlife, Environmental Defense Fund, Federation of Western Outdoor Clubs, Friends of the Earth, Fund for Animals, Izaak Walton League of America, National Audubon Society, National Parks and Conservation Association, National Wildlife Fund, Sierra Club, Wilderness Society, Trout Unlimited, United Auto Workers, and Zero Population Growth.

Many of these environmental groups were held in rather low esteem in Alaska. Throughout the 1980s, many Alaskans remained angry that the federal government, in the Alaska National Interest Lands Conservation Act of 1980 (ANILCA), set aside (or locked up, depending on one's perspective) over 80 million acres of land in national parks, preserves, and monuments, thereby placing it off-limits to oil, gas, mining, and other economic pursuits. Elected officials and organizations from outside Alaska—often pejoratively characterized by Alaskans as "Outside environmental interests"— were behind much of the impetus for these set-asides, and many Alaskans were smarting over this loss. In addition, it was quite difficult for environmental groups to press their claims against oil interests when residents of the state who benefited from oil development were generally supportive of continued oil activity. The Alaska Permanent Fund, which contains nearly $20 billion, is the result of substantial royalties from North Slope oil. Alaskans receive annual checks of approximately $1000; these "dividends" represent part of the investment income of the Permanent Fund. The fund also represents moneys that Alaska will need to withdraw when the oil starts running out early in the next century. Beyond the Permanent Fund, oil money funds airports, schools, cheap and generous student loans, satellite uplink and downlink stations, and numerous public works projects, particularly in rural Alaska.

In sum, until the *Exxon Valdez* spill, it was difficult for environmental groups to be taken seriously in Alaska. While the environmental movement was gaining in stature nationwide, there had never been an environmental catastrophe on the scale of the *Exxon Valdez* to rouse Alaskans to question the assurances of the oil companies. Such events are crucial to recruiting new members to environmental groups, particularly since the benefits to members that accrue from joining such groups can enhance feelings of political efficacy in the wake of a disaster (McCann 1986).

While environmental groups had a difficult time winning Alaskans over to their position, the Cordova Fisheries Union was held in reasonably high esteem by those Alaskans who followed the fishing industry.

Fishing has long been an important industry in Alaska and was the number one industry in southeastern Alaska during territorial days. Only the oil boom of the late 1960s toppled fishing from its central position in the Alaskan economy. But thousands of Alaskans depended on the fishery for their livelihood, and their livelihoods were directly endangered by the *Exxon Valdez* spill.

The Valdez accident was a galvanizing event for the environmental community, which in this case very prominently includes the fishing industry. "Tim Mahoney, a spokesman for the Alaska Coalition and a strong critic of ANWR [Arctic National Wildlife Refuge][3] drilling, said the spill prompted 'furious' calls to his and other organizations. 'This has tapped a nerve in the country that I've never witnessed,' he said" (Congressional Quarterly 1989a, 678). Phone calls to environmental groups and to elected officials, donations to environmental organizations, and new memberships in these groups increased markedly after the *Exxon Valdez* spill. Most environmental groups avidly used the images of the spill and the damage done as graphic elements of their appeals to potential new members. Still, the spill was not *planned* (and certainly not hoped for) by environmental groups, which were no more prepared initially for the spill and the postspill debate than were Exxon or its allies. The balance of power between oil and the environment, by default, tilts in favor of the considerable resources and political clout, at the state and federal levels, of the oil industry. However, the *Exxon Valdez* altered the balance. Environmental groups could use symbols to condense the spill into very few images (oiled sea otters, dead birds, workers cleaning oiled rocks with Handi-Wipes). These images trumped the symbol-poor arguments of the oil industry that the spill was not serious and that it would be cleaned up right away.

The fishers were also mobilized by the spill. In the near term, they acted to protect their interests. They immediately boomed off the areas around fish hatcheries they had founded with state money (ironically made possible by oil revenues). They took their boats out to survey the extent of the spill and to provide an alternative to reports issued by Exxon, Alyeska, and the Coast Guard. They also engaged in a political campaign to reinforce their position that oil and fisheries do not coexist well, particularly in the wake of a large oil spill.

The fishers' cause was advanced not only by the fact of the spill and the power of the symbols surrounding it, but also by the presence of an intelligent, articulate, and credible spokesperson for their cause. This spokesperson, Rikki Ott, is a Cordova fisher and community leader who also holds a doctorate in marine biology from the University of Washington. Ott appeared several times in the media and before state and federal legislative hearings to discuss the impact of the spill on the fishing industry and to remind policy makers of their promises of a safe system for transporting oil in Prince William Sound. Exxon and its allies had a number of equally expert spokespeople, and their spill cleanup effort registered some minor victories. But their inept public relations response in the days following the event could not match the fishers' moral force. Still, we cannot blame the power of oil spills simply on oil companies' fumbling responses to these events. The symbolic power of oil spills is considerable, as I take up in the next section.

THE SYMBOLIC POWER OF OIL SPILLS

The symbolic power of oil spills is undeniable. "Oil spills are one of the most highly visible and emotion-causing forms of ocean pollution" (Interagency Committee on Ocean Pollution Research 1981, 76–77). Most people can recall the images of major oil spills in the 1960s, 1970s, and 1980s: black, gooey oil washing up ashore, oiled wildlife, futile efforts to clean up the spill, and arguments about what to do about the spill.

The first powerful demonstration of the symbolic power of the aftermath of an oil spill was in Santa Barbara. Television beamed images of oiled beaches, birds, and people throughout the United States. Images of gooey spill victims were particularly dramatic and were reinforced with widespread coverage of the volume of oil spilled and the reaction of the local community. Of particular note was the debate between Union Oil Company, the owner of the well, and environmentalists and Santa Barbarans over who was to blame for the spill (Potter 1973).

The dominant symbols of the *Exxon Valdez* spill were of oiled otters and birds, the soiling of the "pristine Alaskan environment," and the image of a large, uncaring oil company, which employed a drunk tanker captain, spilled oil, and then failed to manage the cleanup. The symbols and imagery of these oil spills do not, by themselves, carry much weight. Rather, the symbols need to be carried beyond the most immediately affected group of people to a broader group, the attentive public. The primary conduits for the propagation of symbols in American society are the news media, particularly television. "Without the communications media, the spill might never have become a major issue and its consequences might have been negligible" (Easton 1972, 274). Beyond simply transmitting the images to Americans, the images of the spill roused many people to action:

> Television was a powerful factor from the beginning. When viewers saw blue water and white sand smeared with black oil, and birds and people

similarly smeared, their adrenaline began to flow. When they thought
about what they had seen and heard, many of them decided to act (Easton
1972, 275).

Television also became the most important channel through which
the story of the *Exxon Valdez* was told. "Television images of dead
otters and oily birds instantly became archetypes of corporate rapacity
and incompetence, associated Exxon permanently in the public mind
with blackened beaches and drunken sea captains" (Slater 1994, 54).
Such a story was told with relatively little interpretation; the pictures
and the symbols told the story.

The symbolic power of oil spills is exploited by contestants in the
ensuing policy debate through the process of social construction. This
begins immediately after an event. In simplest terms, the disputants
in the debate seek to create a "causal story" to explain why a spill
happened and what should be done about it in the future (Stone 1989).
In industrial accidents like oil spills, the debate is often reduced to a
dispute over whether the event has occurred as an act of human negligence or an act of God that could not be avoided. In the case of the
Santa Barbara blowout, the Union Oil Company immediately sought
to blame the blowout on natural forces. "The basic cause of the spill,
[a Union spokesman] claimed, was that 'mother nature had let us down'
by letting oil out of the drilling sands." Environmentalists, claiming that
"Union had injured 'Mother Nature' enough without adding insult by
blaming her for not putting down enough casing," suggested that
willful negligence was at the heart of the spill (Potter 1973, 168–69).

Another way of constructing an event was to deny that the event
was a disaster at all. The president of Union Oil tried this tactic, noting
that while the spill was "referred to as a disaster, it is not a disaster
to people. There is no one being killed" (Potter 1973, 69). This construction was of course furiously disputed by environmentalists, and the
claim did little to enhance Union Oil's public image.[4]

The social construction process after the *Exxon Valdez* spill was
similar, from the perspective of the oil company and environmentalists.
Exxon took three routes to explaining the accident. The company initially argued that the spill was an act of God, as the calving of icebergs
off nearby glaciers forced the *Exxon Valdez* to make the fateful turn
that put her off course and into the rocks. This contention was found
wanting when it was revealed that the ship was avoiding "icebergs"
that were of little threat to the ship. Even so, the channel was so wide
that the icebergs and the reef could be avoided easily. Exxon's next
tactic was to place primary blame for the spill on the *Exxon Valdez*'s
captain, Joseph Hazelwood. Captain Hazelwood was found to be le-

gally intoxicated when the ship left Port Valdez, was not on the bridge when the grounding occurred, and had left the helm to a third mate who was not certified to take the helm in Prince William Sound. This attempt at blame shifting was countered by environmentalists and their allies, who asserted that Exxon knew of the captain's drinking problem, and that, in any case, Captain Hazelwood's drunkenness did not absolve Exxon of corporate responsibility (a conclusion reached by the courts as well).

So important was the imagery of the *Exxon Valdez* spill, and so inept was the corporate response, that two analysts of corporate communications called the spill a public relations nightmare and crisis management failure for Exxon. Exxon violated basic tenets of effective crisis communication and management, and thus lost the war of symbols, at least in the near term (Williams and Treadaway 1992). In Exxon's defense, however, there are elements of this and any large oil spill that should be acknowledged. First, the spill was so large and so unexpected that any organization's initial response to the spill could be expected to be faltering. The Coast Guard, the state of Alaska, and the Alyeska Pipeline Service Company (the owner of the pipeline) were all targets of and participants in blame fixing. All these actions were dutifully reported by the news media (Smith 1992, 9).

Compounding Exxon's public relations problems was the special symbolic value of Alaska. Alaska conjures a series of images in most Americans' minds about a wild, pristine, isolated, scenically beautiful place that, consonant with the slogan "The Last Frontier," is largely untouched by humans. The oil industry had long promoted this image, along with promoting the notion that oil exploration is compatible with the preservation of the Alaskan environment. When the *Exxon Valdez* ran aground, the public was confronted with evidence that oil transportation was not necessarily compatible with the preservation of Alaskan scenic and environmental assets.

As in the Santa Barbara spill, the *Exxon Valdez* gained a great deal of its symbolic power through the propagation of images by the news media, particularly television (Jones 1989; Slater 1994; Smith 1992). Many of the images of the spill—in particular, oiled wildlife and fishers frantically seeking to boom off hatcheries and clean equipment—become so powerful because they were constantly reinforced by pack journalism practices. Pack journalism encourages uniform coverage of events by all journalists; privileges standard, culturally acceptable sources that tend to provide "news" to journalists; and subordinates news that derives from unofficial sources or that expresses viewpoints at variance with the established story line (Bennett 1995). In the *Exxon Valdez* spill, the official sources were the Coast Guard, oil companies, leaders of mainstream environmental groups, and, to a much smaller extent, spokespeople for the fishers. Many of these spokespersons for the fishers were fishers themselves. They often preferred to spend their time trying to mitigate the damage from the spill rather than adding their spin to the news about the spill (Slater 1994; Smith 1992).

The imagery of the *Argo Merchant* spill was not as vivid as that of the *Exxon Valdez* or Santa Barbara spills, because the *Argo Merchant* went aground offshore, in international waters, on a shallow bar near Nantucket Island, Massachusetts. Much of the oil spilled into the open ocean, rather than into a bay or estuary. While spills in the open ocean are relatively rare, the spill pitted various interests against each other to depict the spill in a manner consistent with contending group interests. The construction of the spill ran to two basic themes. The first theme is a familiar one: the alleged negligence of the captain and crew. It was alleged that the crew had turned off its depth finder and other navigational equipment, and that the captain was asleep when the ship ran aground (Kifner 1976; *New York Times* 1976).

The second theme was that foreign-owned and -registered tankers follow less stringent safety requirements than American ships. In particular, concern was raised that the *Argo Merchant* and other ships registered under the Liberian "flag of convenience," such as the *Olympic Games*, which spilled oil in the Delaware River on December 27, 1976, were evading international norms of safety (e.g. Congressional Quarterly 1977b). Both these claims were denied by shipping and oil interests, as well as by the *Argo Merchant's* captain.

In all these spills, and numerous smaller ones, the pattern in the days after the spill is similar. Both advocacy coalitions—the environmental and the oil company camps—immediately seek to gain the rhetorical high ground. In all these cases, however, it is very difficult for the oil industry and its allies to prevail in the immediate term. After all, against a background of statistics, technical reports, and claims that the long-run safety of oil transportation is sound are arrayed much more comprehensible, much more emotionally charged images of the most recent big spill. As Molotch and Lester (1975) note, an oil spill of considerable magnitude is very difficult to conceal and manage— the spill, in essence, is impossible to ignore. The best one can do is try to contain the controversy surrounding the spill or construct the story of the spill in such a way as to minimize the political damage resulting from it.

POLICY OUTCOMES OF OIL SPILLS

I make no claim that policy change is a necessary outgrowth of agenda change, either by way of focusing events or otherwise. Yet it is possible to isolate examples of policy change that occurred after major oil spills. Again, the examples I use are the Santa Barbara, *Argo Merchant*, and *Exxon Valdez* spills.

In the Santa Barbara spill, the hopes of environmentalists and community activists were tempered by the knowledge that Secretary of the Interior Walter Hickel was not generally kindly disposed to environmental interests. Hickel, a former (and future) governor of Alaska, was closely associated with oil interests and with development generally. Still, the magnitude of the Santa Barbara spill, and the fact that little if any attention had ever been paid to federal policy regarding offshore oil development, induced the secretary to issue a temporary moratorium on new leases in the Santa Barbara channel. So little attention had been paid to offshore leasing that "in Washington, New Jersey's Senator Clifford Case expressed shock on learning that there had never been a public hearing on an offshore oil drilling lease request. He urged Hickel to hold public hearings before granting any more offshore leases" (Steinhart and Steinhart 1972, 54). This moratorium was short-lived and fell far short of the environmentalists' goal to prohibit any future lease sales in the channel. Indeed,

> Secretary Hickel's announcement that the Interior Department was generating new 'tough' regulations to control off-shore drilling was met with considerable skepticism. The Santa Barbara County Board of Supervisors was invited to "review" these new regulations and refused to do so in the belief that such participation would be used to provide a false impression of democratic responsiveness (Molotch 1970, 92).

Clearly, the new regulations and the moratorium on drilling were the result of the spill and can be labeled, at a minimum, transient policy changes.

In the immediate term, the state of California also took action after the spill. As Steinhart and Steinhart explain:

> There was an anxious period of self-examination and reexamination at all governmental levels which began as soon as news of the oil leak was received. In Sacramento, Governor Ronald Reagan immediately ordered all state agencies involved with offshore leases to review their regulations, to assure that no similar incident could occur on state owned lands. At the same time, Representative Charles Teague told the press that Secretary Hickel was already reviewing the federal regulations and that he suspected that they were not as strict as they should be (Steinhart and Steinhart 1972, 49).

In the longer term, some policy change resulted that would have been unlikely to occur without this spill. The two primary legislative changes were the Ports and Waterways Safety Act (P.L. 92-340) and the Federal Water Pollution Control Act (FWPCA). The former authorizes federal agencies to control vessels in a manner similar to air traffic control. This act was folded into the Port and Tanker Safety Act of 1978 (P.L. 95-500), which was itself a product of the short period of heightened concern after the *Argo Merchant* oil spill.

The primary feature of the FWPCA (later the Clean Water Act) was its provision calling for the establishment of a National Oil and Hazardous Substances Pollution Contingency Plan. The key provision in the oil spill field is the creation of the spiller's liability for restoration and cleanup under Section 311 of the act, with the federal government monitoring cleanup when the spiller cannot or will not undertake the task or when the spill is deemed to be an act of God (Interagency Committee on Ocean Pollution Research 1981, 76–80). This latter provision not only makes it good politics for oil companies to argue that oil spills are acts of God—it makes good legal and economic sense, from the spiller's perspective, to press the argument as well.

While these provisions were important changes in the law, this policy change is not solely the result of focusing events and their influence on oil spill policy was limited. First, this legislation was not merely the result of the Santa Barbara oil spill, but was instead a response to a number of environmental issues and problems that were revealed in the late 1960s and early 1970s, including oil and hazardous materials spills. Second, the federal government's role as overseer and cleanup contractor of last resort clearly placed the federal government in the role of cleaning up messes caused by others.

The *Argo Merchant* oil spill was also followed by a flurry of legislative activity, culminating in the Port and Tanker Safety Act. The *Congressional Quarterly Weekly Report* traced the fate of legislation addressing oil spills throughout 1977 and that year's *Congressional Quarterly Almanac* noted explicitly that proposals were made in response to the *Argo Merchant* spill (Congressional Quarterly 1977b, 668). However, it must be noted that the resulting legislation was nowhere near as stringent as had been hoped for by environmentalists and their allies. The enactment finally passed by Congress—the Port and Tanker Safety Act—did not address broader issues of spill prevention and liability. Comprehensive legislation to deal with liability died for two reasons: the combining of chemical spills with oil spills for the purposes of drafting a liability law and the failure of legislators to agree on whether state laws on oil spills should be preempted by a uniform federal statute. Preemption pitted representatives, many of whom were supported by oil and chemical interests and therefore supported preemption of state laws, against senators from coastal states who wished to retain their liability and compensation systems. The preemption issue was to be the major obstacle to liability reform for over 13 years, until the *Exxon Valdez* tipped the balance against preemption.

Between the *Argo Merchant* and the *Exxon Valdez*, Congress revisited the oil spill issue nearly every year. In the early years of this campaign, efforts were made to combine oil spills and chemical spills liability and compensation into one comprehensive program. This program eventually became the Superfund system of chemical dump cleanups, but oil spills were detached from this program because oil and chemical interests did not want to pay for each others' spills. Once the Superfund was enacted and the memory of the *Argo Merchant* and other spills faded, the momentum to pass oil spill legislation was lost. The preemption issue was so daunting that by the mid-1980s it was rare for both houses to pass a version of an oil spill liability scheme.

The urgency to pass oil spill legislation was renewed by the *Exxon Valdez* oil spill. The widespread dismay over this spill was compounded by the realization that policy enacted to prevent or mitigate *Exxon Valdez*-type events was a failure. Under the provisions of the Trans-Alaska Pipeline Authorization Act of 1973 (TAPAA), the pipeline owners were liable for the full costs of controlling and removing any pollution caused by the pipeline. The legislation also established liability without regard to fault of up to $100 million for each incident of oil spills from vessels carrying oil from the pipeline unless the spills were the result of acts of war or actions of the United States. Liability for owners of vessels was limited at $14 million, and a Trans-Alaska Pipeline Liability Fund was established to meet claims of more than $14 million. The fund was financed by a 5-cent fee for each barrel of oil loaded at Port Valdez, but the fund was capped at $100 million.

The failure of this policy became evident soon after the spill. Environmentalists and fishers sought to invoke the provisions of the TAPAA and require the owners of the Trans-Alaska Pipeline (TAP) to pay a portion of the damages, since it could be argued that the spill was a consequence of the operation of the pipeline. This claim was never effectively pressed. The second failure was in the liability provisions and the limits on liability. A $100 million cap was found to be woefully inadequate to pay for cleanup and compensation of the victims of the oil spill, in this case, the fishing industry and Native Alaskan villages in the Sound. The $14 million limit on liability for the shipowner was also extremely low. In the end the amounts paid out by Exxon for compensation, cleanup costs, and legal fees and damages exceeded $2 billion, far greater than the limits provided for under the TAPAA. The third failure of policy was signified by the oil spill itself. Environmentalists and some Alaskans, particularly those living near the Sound, had opposed the TAP, fearing environmental damage from a large spill. Their concerns were supposedly addressed by a legislative mandate that care be taken to protect the environment in the construction and operation of the pipeline and in the shipping of oil. In exchange for assurances that environmental concerns would be taken seriously, Congress exempted the TAP project from the National Environmental Policy Act.

The immediate policy effect of the *Exxon Valdez* spill was to prevent the opening of the Arctic National Wildlife Refuge (ANWR) to oil exploration (Satchell and Carpenter 1989, 62). While the Iraqi invasion of Kuwait in 1990 somewhat restored the chances of ANWR being reopened, as of this writing ANWR is still off-limits to oil and gas exploration, due in large part to the blow to oil's credibility following the oil spill.

The longer-term policy effect of the spill was to provide the impetus for the Oil Pollution Act (OPA) of 1990. It seems quite clear that were it not for the *Exxon Valdez* oil spill, Congress might still be deadlocked over this issue. With the preemption issue swept away by the spill, public anger very high, and Congress determined to do something about oil spills, the Oil Pollution Act of 1990 was nearly inevitable. But the OPA was not drafted in a vacuum. Rather, the legislation was the result of years of debate followed by the balance tipping radically in favor of change as a result of a particularly dramatic and troubling accident.

Finally, the oil companies did learn important technical and political lessons from oil spills. Their spill-driven innovations may not have been achieved without prodding from these events. These lessons include improved techniques for loading and unloading oil, better ship-construction techniques (also spurred by the OPA), improved training, drug and alcohol screening, and improved deployment of ships and equipment to respond to oil spills. However, some of these lessons have as much to do with public relations and issue containment as with improved technologies and cleanup plans. As one reporter noted, the drills that oil companies hold to prepare for oil spills "give company flacks the opportunity to practice varnishing the truth in case the mop-up doesn't go as planned" (Satchell and Carpenter 1989, 54).

CONCLUSIONS

In chapter 3, I showed how the influence of an event on the congressional agenda is conditioned by the nature of the policy domain in which the problem is located. The oil spill domain is characterized by group conflict, which is reflected in the agenda dynamics of this domain. The style of group conflict, the nature of group participation, and the policy area in which oil spill policy is embedded further support this proposition. The oil spill story provides an outstanding opportunity to understand how groups seek to contain and expand issues, and how such activities must take into account broader issues in environmental politics.

The history of environmental politics since the 1960s has been characterized by considerable group conflict. Environmental protection is a highly emotional issue, not only for those who wish to see the environment protected. Elected officials, bureaucrats, stockholders, executives, and workers also have a stake in decisions to accept a greater or lesser degree of environmental protection. While there may be no essential incompatibility between environmental protection and economic growth in the long run, the perceptions of these issues are often most important in motivating group members and leaders.

Oil spills play an important role in shaping these perceptions. Large spills are portrayed by environmental groups as ecological catastrophes. In spite of some efforts by the oil industry to counter this story, the rich imagery and symbolism of oil spills make issue containment particularly difficult. The news media, on the other hand, are drawn to these stories as dramatic symbols of environmental problems and the conflict between the environment and industry. Once a major spill becomes a major news story, issue containment is virtually impossible.

While a spill is fresh in the public's mind, environmental groups mobilize to add members, raise funds and other resources, and, ultimately, pressure elected officials to change oil spill policy to punish spillers and prevent future spills. The results of such mobilization, as seen in this chapter, are greater institutional attention to oil spills and a greater propensity to legislate in response to oil spills. Consequently there is an active and well-organized environmental community that cannot generally force policy onto the agenda or impose it on the oil industry. In the wake of an oil spill, however, the expansion of the issue, coupled with the change in the presumption against stringent environmental regulation, provides a window of opportunity for new oil spill policy that would not exist without these events.

5

Nuclear Power Plant Accidents as Focusing Events

In this chapter I consider safety-related incidents, problems, mishaps, and accidents at nuclear power plants. The problems of nuclear power are considerably different from those raised by earthquakes, hurricanes, or oil spills, and the politics of nuclear power reflect its unique status in energy policy and in public policy making more broadly. Nuclear power is not sprung on humanity through some natural process, like the weather or movement of the earth's crust. Nor was nuclear power gradually harnessed during the industrial revolution, as were fossil fuels. Rather, nuclear power in the United States was initially developed through the efforts of a government racing desperately against an enemy in war to produce the most destructive weapon in human history. This research and development effort—the Manhattan Project—culminated in the first wartime use of nuclear bombs in August 1945. The association of nuclear power with nearly instantaneous destruction hangs over nuclear physics and the civilian nuclear power industry to this day.

Having spent over $2 billion in 1940s dollars (over $10 billion in 1995 dollars) to build the atomic bomb, the United States government sought to harness the atom for "peaceful" ends. The Atomic Era promised to usher in a new age, in which energy would be plentiful, clean, and "too cheap to meter."[1] But the technology was so new, expensive, and dangerous that it required government promotion and intervention to develop as a civilian industry. The nuclear industry was created, financed, promoted, and underwritten by the federal government and a vast scientific, technical, academic, and military infrastructure. Nuclear power was not to be an ordinary industry.

Nor was nuclear technology simply another futuristic "high-tech" innovation that was oversold by its proponents and then faded away as it failed to deliver on its promise. Within thirty years of the advent of this technology and twenty years after its first civilian application, very serious doubts began to set in as to the safety and economics of nuclear power. The technology has always been so exotic, so uniquely dangerous, and so closely connected with the history of nuclear weapons production that highly unusual governmental structures were created to promote and oversee it. The federal government has had to induce private-sector investment in it, most notably through its programs to limit liability to power plant owners and contractors.

In the 1960s, many policy decisions regarding public/private participation in nuclear power had been settled and nuclear power plant building continued rapidly. As part of this building program, the nuclear establishment assured the public that nuclear power was not only safe but was also an example of American technical prowess and "progress" (Gamson and Modigliani 1989). By the 1970s, however, nuclear power had become by far the most costly and the most controversial form of energy used in the United States. An entire social movement rose up to oppose nuclear power plant construction, licensing, and operation. Even before this movement gained strength, the technical problems inherent in nuclear power made it far more expensive than traditional fossil fuels. And although the Three Mile Island (TMI) accident did not greatly accelerate trends away from the further expansion of nuclear power (those trends had begun years earlier), it did focus mass public attention on safety, cost, and nuclear waste issues associated with civilian nuclear power plants. It therefore was a significant contributor to the decay of confidence in nuclear power in the United States. In that sense, TMI was clearly a focusing event. However, in stark contrast to the domains considered in chapters 3 and 4, there are few other major accidents in the period of this study. Nuclear power in the United States is a one-event domain, and I find that the hypothesized political relationships introduced in chapter 2 and tested with generally good results in chapters 3 and 4 do not relate as strongly to agenda activity in the nuclear power domain.

MODELS AND DATA

The analysis begins with the models, which reveal how TMI is the sole event of note in this domain. The models and variables in this section are similar to those presented in the previous chapters. The individual focusing events are less obvious in nuclear power because, unlike the natural disaster or oil spill cases, there has not been one civilian nuclear power accident in the United States than can absolutely be said to have led to a loss of life. Property damage is also an unsuitable criterion for isolating important incidents, as the damage to property as a result of these accidents does not extend beyond the facility. Using this as an indicator of the size or importance of a nuclear accident would be akin to counting the value of a ship lost in an oil spill as the measure of the magnitude of an oil spill.

The task here is to study events that are selected on consistently applied criteria for their inclusion in the data set. Congress recognized the need for information on the potential dangers of nuclear power (many of which are freely admitted by the nuclear industry) and required the NRC, under the Energy Reorganization Act of 1974, to supply to Congress a "Quarterly Report on Abnormal Occurrences" (hereinafter Abnormal Occurrence Reports, or AORs)[2] (e.g., Nuclear Regulatory Commission 1994). Most of these abnormal occurrences happen at individual plants, although some are "generic" problems shared by all reactors or by reactors of a particular design. In the data set based on these AORs there were 69 abnormal occurrences between 1979 and 1990. Generic occurrences were not included because they cannot be fixed to a particular place or time. The vast majority of abnormal occurrences are relatively minor. They are notable only because they occur in operating *nuclear* power plants, where the potential for disaster is so great (Perrow 1984, chapter 1). However, some abnormal occurrences become the subject of significant attention from the NRC and sometimes from Congress.

NRC also includes follow-ups to previous AORs in the reports to provide Congress with ongoing information beyond the initial report of an incident. Since no accidents in this data set resulted in loss of life or in property damage beyond that which may have occurred at the plant, these follow-up reports provide the best available means for measuring the "seriousness" of a nuclear incident, as determined through the expert application of consistent criteria. For each event in the data set I counted how many times the NRC followed up on the event in their reports to Congress. I assert that the more serious the accident, the greater the need for continual NRC scrutiny of the utility's response to the accident, as reflected in the follow-up reports. By this criterion, the TMI accident, which is mentioned most often by witnesses in the domain and which was discussed by the NRC in subsequent reports 41 times, is by far the most serious event in the data set.

In the following models, the rarity of the event is the number of days that have passed since the last event of similar magnitude, based on the seriousness measure. The rarity value of the TMI accident is based on the number of days between the accident and the accident at the Tennessee Valley Authority's plant at Browns Ferry, Alabama, in March 1975. Browns Ferry is considered to be among the most serious nuclear accidents in the history of civilian nuclear power before TMI (Comey 1979).

These tables differ slightly from those shown in chapters 3 and 4. I show two models, one that includes the TMI accident and one that does not, to isolate the effect that the outlying case, the TMI accident, has on the congressional agenda in the domain.[3] In Table 5-1, the effect of the TMI accident on the models is clear. TMI is the outlying case in the analysis, and its inclusion in the model, even where variables are transformed to conform more closely to a normal distribution, results in inflated R^2 values. Conversely, the exclusion of the TMI incident from the model results in models with low correlation coefficients and insignificant regression models. The conclusion I reach is that the TMI accident is a singular event, and the effect of other smaller and less well-known events is considerably more ambiguous. The result of this analysis suggests that TMI is the only truly focal event of note in this domain in the period of the study. Even so, its focusing power is ambiguous.

Table 5-2 is the model of the influence of political attributes of the postevent period on congressional agenda change. The only political attribute that is significantly related to congressional agenda activity is news coverage. None of the other political variables significantly influence the congressional agenda. The fact that the news is the only attribute related to congressional agenda activity suggests that the news' relationship with the congressional agenda may have more to do with coincidence in time than with a systemic relationship in which news coverage drives congressional agenda change.

TABLE 5-1 Event Attribute Models

| | Correlation Coefficients | | | |
| | News Agenda Activity | | Congressional Agenda Activity | |
	With TMI	Without TMI	With TMI	Without TMI
Damage	0.547	0.092	0.516	0.215
Rarity	0.248	−0.012	0.220	0.027
Scope	0.050	0.049	0.032	0.025
	Regression Results[a]			
Adjusted R^2	0.293	0.000	0.261	0.022
F	10.407	0.388	9.023	1.501
p	0.000	0.762	0.000	0.223
N	69	68	69	68

[a]Dependent variables are news and congressional agenda activity, respectively. Variables are transformed to meet the requirements of OLS regression. Variables are defined in the text and the methodological appendix.

TABLE 5-2 Political Model of the Congressional Agenda

Standardized Regression Coefficients

	Congressional Agenda Activity	
	With TMI	*Without TMI*
News Change	0.752**	0.804**
News Density	0.221**	−0.022
Mobilization	−0.074	−0.068
Scope	0.052	−0.034
Mean Tone	0.098	0.123
Adjusted R^2	0.705	0.591
F	33.530	20.333
p	0.000	0.000
N	69	68

$^*p<.05$ $^{**}p<.01$

The modeling suggests that there is only one nuclear event that is important in agenda terms—the TMI accident—and that the political attributes of this event and of the minor events in the domain are considerably different from the politics of earthquakes, hurricanes, and oil spills. To understand the reason for this finding, we must delve more deeply into the nature of nuclear power accidents and the policy community in which such accidents are discussed and debated. What is revealed is a domain in which policy making is far more polarized, visible, contentious, and prone to competing interpretations of the meanings of events than in the other domains I study, making events per se less important than in the other cases.

THE POLICY CONTEXT: GOVERNMENT, ENERGY, AND ENVIRONMENT

The federal government has throughout its history promoted private enterprise with subsidies to industry that are often portrayed as public goods. Early policy subsidized roads, canals, and railroads. Fledgling industries such as aircraft and computer technology have also been supported by government purchases, research grants, and regulatory policy. Even so, "the nuclear industry is unique in that the federal government itself is largely responsible for creating as well as sustaining it" (Temples 1980). This section summarizes the history of federal government regulation and promotion of nuclear power.

Government Promotion of Nuclear Power:
From the AEC to the NRC

The story of the harnessing of the atom for nuclear weapons is well-known, culminating in the success of the Manhattan Project in creating atomic bombs in 1945. The nexus between nuclear weapons and peaceful uses of nuclear power was to trouble scientists and government officials from the outset of the nuclear era (Lovins and Lovins 1980; Weingast 1980). Many in government and in the scientific community hoped that this technology could be turned to producing virtually limitless, clean, and cheap energy. The costs of the technology and the inherent dangers of nuclear power required that the government lead research and development of the technology.

Civilian nuclear power was made possible by the Atomic Energy Act of 1947. This legislation created the Atomic Energy Commission and the congressional Joint Committee on Atomic Energy (JCAE), the two primary promoters of civilian nuclear power under the "Atoms for Peace" program. The JCAE was a unique body in the history of the Congress. It was the only joint committee created by statute and was the only joint committee allowed to originate legislation. The committee was widely believed by those inside and outside the legislative branch to be expert in nuclear energy, so much so that it was able to dominate the executive branch in nuclear policy making (Temples 1980, 243). The JCAE served as the cornerstone of a very tightly integrated subgovernment that was very difficult for outsiders, even high officials in the executive branch, to penetrate.

Even with the power of the federal government supporting it, civilian nuclear power developed slowly because of the exotic nature of the technology and uncertainty over the liability of utilities if there is an accident at a nuclear power plant. In response, the government provided an implicit subsidy to the nuclear power industry though the Price Anderson Act of 1957, which capped utility liability for nuclear accidents at $560 million. This act, which was amended with much higher liability limits in 1987, indemnified a broad range of participants in the nuclear power industry and led to the first wave of large-scale civilian power reactor building. An interesting question this raises is, of course, if nuclear power is safe, why do nuclear utilities need to be indemnified (Nader 1979; Temples 1980)?

This system of regulation and promotion of nuclear power remained in place throughout the late 1950s into the early 1970s, when the nuclear subgovernment began showing signs of strain. Nuclear power began to become relatively more expensive than other forms of energy as technical and safety problems emerged. The environmental movement, described in chapter 4, also began to step up its opposition to nuclear power and to engage in grassroots as well as national organizing to block plant licensing and construction. These trends, and the sense of a number of elected officials that a single government agency should not be in the business of both promoting and regulating nuclear power, culminated in the passage of the Atomic Energy Reorganization Act of 1974. This split the AEC into two agencies. The Nuclear Regulatory Commission (NRC) would regulate the safety of nuclear plants. The Energy Research and Development Agency (ERDA) was to provide research support for all energy sources, but in its early days focused almost exclusively on nuclear power. The split of the Atomic Energy Commission into the ERDA and NRC did not yield immediate changes in federal attitudes and policies toward nuclear power. "The NRC staff was reincarnated from the AEC, and the NRC's first official act was to adopt all of the AEC's rules and regulations" (Weiss 1979, 41).

The reorganization of the nuclear regulatory regime in the United States coincided with the "Energy Crisis" of the mid-1970s. Oil prices quadrupled, supplies were cut for political reasons, and all energy prices sharply increased. Nuclear power was touted as a way of improving American energy self-sufficiency, a theme that nuclear power proponents continue to sound today (Gamson and Modigliani 1989). Nuclear power was a crucial part of President Ford's energy plans, in which he stated a goal of between 200 and 240 nuclear generating stations in the United States by 1985 (Congressional Quarterly 1975, 277–78). That level was never reached, with plants peaking at 111 operable plants in 1992 (United States Department of Commerce 1993, table 960). While the United States has a greater electrical generating capacity from nuclear power than any other western nation, the nuclear share of total electrical power is lower than France, which continues with a vigorous nuclear program. Other factors, such as conservation in response to higher energy prices, slowed the growth of energy usage in the United States so that predicted electrical power shortages did not develop, thereby making nuclear power less attractive.

The economic downturn of the 1970s, the oil embargo, and increased interest in coal and nuclear power (both of which have serious environmental consequences) caused the environmental movement to lose some ground, and it thereby lost its clout in opposing nuclear power and other environmentally hazardous sources of energy. Even so, the environmental community retained enough influence, and enough clout was gained through new federal laws such as the National Environmental Policy Act (NEPA), to allow the movement to continue to pressure the nuclear industry.

The Collapse of the Nuclear Subgovernment

The collapse of the nuclear subgovernment is rooted in the growing economic problems of nuclear power; the breakup of the AEC; the elimination of the JCAE in 1977; the creation of the Department of Energy (DOE), which absorbed ERDA in 1977; and the previously discussed antinuclear movement. The JCAE was abolished

> because of the general perception that the committee members were too close to the industry. A number of congressional committees claimed responsibility for oversight. Venue shopping clearly played an important role in this process, and its importance was understood by those on both sides. Opponents followed the classic pattern of expanding the conflict by altering its institutional venue. . . .
>
> When the industry lost control of the issue, when the venue had been expanded by opponents to include licensing, oversight, and rate making, the future was determined. Utilities ordered only fifteen more plants after 1974. Opponents had won primarily by getting their vision of the issue accepted and by altering the nature of the decision-making process by expanding the range of participants involved (Baumgartner and Jones 1993, 69–70).

Further evidence of the demise of nuclear power, but also evidence of its considerable political staying power, is provided by the demise of the Clinch River Breeder Reactor project in the late 1970s. The Clinch River project was special in that it created as much fuel—plutonium— as it consumed, promising a limitless source of energy. The nuclear industry heralded it as the energy source of the future, but antinuclear advocates opposed the plants, asserting that creating so much plutonium would make the plant a potential target for nuclear terrorists and would undermine world efforts at controlling the proliferation of nuclear weapons and weapons-grade fuel. These concerns, as well as extremely high costs and active opposition from the Natural Resources Defense Council (NRDC), caused President Carter to kill funds for the project by vetoing the 1977 energy research bill (Congressional Quarterly 1977a, 683). Congressional proponents, however, fought vigorously for the project until the early 1980s, when political support and momentum for the project decayed, in large part as a result of the TMI accident.

Environmentalism and the Antinuclear Movement

Baumgartner and Jones assert that "ultimately, nuclear power was abandoned in the United States because the industry became uncompetitive with alternative sources of energy. The financial plight of the nuclear power industry occurred during a period of long-term problems in the electric power industry" (1993, 76). In this view, the environmental and antinuclear movement was a relatively less important factor in the erosion of confidence in nuclear power. Unfavorable economics were certainly important, but interest group activity was still very important in explaining policy outcomes in this domain. The environmental movement was active, vocal, and successful in opening the domain to scrutiny, which led to greater debate and wider public concern. This, in turn, led to safety demands or outright opposition to power plants in particular areas, which drove up costs even further. Although antinuclear groups have declined in influence since the early 1980s, the legacy of their activism and the contradictions of nuclear power itself have combined to undermine nuclear power as an important energy source in the United States.

The antinuclear movement in the United States consists of three types of groups. The first type is the technical community, whose interest in the safety of nuclear power predates the birth of the environmental movement. This expert community is led by the Union of Concerned Scientists (UCS), an organization founded by MIT graduate students and faculty in 1969 out of concern over the arms race and nuclear proliferation (Joppke 1993, 29). Its main concern has traditionally been nuclear weapons; however, the UCS historically devotes about 25 percent of its resources to lobbying for more stringent nuclear power regulation. UCS has consistently opposed nuclear plant standardization proposals, urges that plants be allowed to operate only when a state emergency plan is in place, and lobbies to encourage development of alternative energy sources. The credibility of the UCS, which has been called "the most highly respected of the groups criticizing the industry" (Congressional Quarterly 1979, 693), was greatly enhanced by the protest resignation of Robert Pollard, a respected nuclear engineer, from the NRC in 1976 and his joining the UCS a short time later (Temples 1980, 252). Pollard is a perennial witness at hearings on nuclear power. Many other members of the UCS are former industry, AEC, or NRC employees who joined the UCS when they questioned their industry's claims of safety.

Apart from the UCS, others have provided technical expertise to counter the claims of the utilities, reactor makers, and the AEC/NRC. Academics not associated with UCS, as well as whistle-blowers who have resigned from public and private-sector promoters of nuclear energy, have also lent their expertise to the debate. It is very difficult for the nuclear power industry to dismiss these technical experts as dilettantes, troublemakers, or environmental extremists.

The technical expertise represented by UCS and scientific and technical experts led to early successes in delaying the licensing and operation of nuclear plants that were allegedly unsafe. The early 1970s saw the formation of the Consolidated National Intervenors (CNI). This group "was formed to participate in the ECCS [Emergency Core Cooling System] hearings,"[4] and "comprised sixty local and national groups ranging from the UCS, the Sierra Club, and the Chicago-based Businessmen in the Public Interest to local citizens groups. . . ." (Joppke 1993, 30). While the CNI did not oppose nuclear power per se, it did seek to make the technology safer. To do so, they focused their energies on the licensing process, to slow the construction of new plants and to ensure, to the greatest extent possible, that safety issues were addressed. The results were dramatic. "Between 1962 and 1966, only 12 percent of all license applications were legally contested by local citizen groups. Between 1967 and 1971, the rate of intervention was already 32 percent. From 1970 to 1972, local intervenors challenged no less than 73 percent of all applications reviewed in AEC hearings" (ibid.). Intervention in the licensing hearing process, and the technical support provided by UCS and its scientific allies, thus forced the industry for the first time to take into account local safety concerns that were buttressed by technically competent commentary and analysis.

The second important type of groups involved in the antinuclear movement are the national environmental and public-interest organizations. These include "the Sierra Club, Friends of the Earth, the Natural Resources Defense Council, the Scientists' Institute for Public Information, and the Committee for Nuclear Responsibility, along with such prominent individuals as consumer advocate Ralph Nader and scientists Barry Commoner, John Gofman, Arthur Tamplin, Harold Urey, George Wald, Linus Pauling, and George Kistiakowsky" (Temples 1980, 247). The Friends of the Earth (FOE), which was founded by a former member of the Sierra Club who found their tactics insufficiently aggressive, was among the first major environmentalist groups to take an active role in opposing nuclear power, dating their involvement in antinuclear issues to 1970.

Increasing opposition to nuclear power, like the strong reactions against oil spills, can be traced to the growth of the environmental movement in the early 1970s. This movement, as described in chapter 4, was galvanized, as Joppke (1993) reminds us, by the Santa Barbara oil spill of 1969 and coalesced around the symbol of Earth Day 1970. The increase in interest in the environment led to rapid increases in membership in mainstream conservation organizations. The Sierra Club and the Audubon Society, for example, experienced nearly fourfold growth between 1960 and 1970. But perhaps more important, the increase in environmental consciousness "became institutionalized in a new brand of environmental organizations," which combined a spirited activism with "rigorous expert professionalism and a high emphasis on lobbying and litigation" (Joppke 1993, 31–32). It was this newly aggressive element of the environmental movement that pressed the case against nuclear energy.

A critical event in the history of the antinuclear movement was the formation of Ralph Nader's Critical Mass Alliance in 1974 (Jasper 1988). This group was very important for three reasons. First, as the Atomic Industrial Forum noted, "the antinuclear movement has crystal-lized under its own banner. It has shed the environmentalist image which it carried for several years and is now a full-fledged political movement" (quoted in Joppke 1993, 63). The movement thus became a stand-alone social movement rather than simply a subset of the environmental movement. Second, and related to this, the Critical Mass movement was intended to work as a public-interest group, as opposed to the more elite, professional NRDC, Sierra Club, or UCS (ibid.).

This populist orientation led to the creation of additional local citizen-led groups that opposed the construction and licensing of plants in their communities. Among the best known of these groups was the Clamshell Alliance, which very vigorously opposed the opening of the Seabrook plant in New Hampshire. The Abalone Alliance fought nuclear power plants in California, including the infamous Diablo Canyon plant, known for its design flaws and alleged inadequate seismic design. Local groups and governmental leaders on Long Island, New York, successfully prevented the poorly sited Shoreham nuclear plant (in the middle of densely populated Long Island) from operating.

John Kingdon notes that focusing events are but one way that "windows of opportunity" open to invite increased political participation, change the agenda, and perhaps result in policy change (Kingdon 1995). He further notes that such windows are fleeting, and that the opportunity to affect the agenda will close fairly quickly if groups fail to exploit it. In this case, the birth and growth of the antinuclear movement in the early and mid-1970s made available substantial resources to react to the TMI accident. These groups' efforts peaked with a post-TMI demonstration in New York in which 200,000 people joined. Some of the vigor of the antinuclear power movement waned, however, as concern over nuclear weapons grew in the early 1980s and activists moved into the peace movement (Jasper 1988). This shift to the peace movement troubled many local antinuclear activists, many of whose members were politically moderate or even conservative, but who opposed nuclear plants in their communities (Joppke 1993). The connections between local groups that opposed specific plants and larger groups with a broader social or environmental agenda were loosened, and the cohesiveness of the movement decayed. Still, the groundwork had been laid for local efforts to oppose nuclear power. This describes the Shoreham controversy, where local residents and governments opposed the plant and its owner, Long Island Lighting Company (LILCO), for years. They finally forced LILCO and the state of New York to develop a plan to decommission the plant before it was placed in commercial operation.

Nuclear Policy in 1979

By 1979 the groundwork had been laid for the intensified debate over nuclear power that would be fueled by the TMI accident. As discussed, the antinuclear movement was in full swing, with environmental groups, antinuclear public-interest groups, and local antinuclear and intervenor groups pressing their case against nuclear power. Meanwhile, the nuclear industry was reeling but not defeated. The major industry groups—including the Atomic Industrial Forum and the Edison Electric Institute; contractors such as the major makers of nuclear reactors (Babcock and Wilcox, Combustion Engineering, General Electric, and Westinghouse); and major nuclear electric utilities, both public and private, such as Consolidated Edison (ConEd), Long Island Lighting Company, and the Tennessee Valley Authority (TVA)—continued to press for legislative and political support of nuclear power. They were beginning to make some legislative gains in the late 1970s. Although President Carter (notably, a former naval nuclear engineer) continually opposed the Clinch River Breeder Reactor, he did not foreclose more conventional nuclear power as an important energy source. This position was driven by the oil price shock of the late 1970s, when Iranian oil supplies became unreliable and energy prices again skyrocketed. In light of national energy needs and demands from the nuclear power industry for regulatory relief, the president proposed legislation in 1978 that would have streamlined licensing procedures for nuclear power plants and, in particular, would have streamlined siting decisions and would have limited opportunities for intervenors to block plants. This began a very heated debate over how and to what extent citizens could participate in these siting decisions.

Well before TMI, the domain was highly polarized between pronuclear groups and antinuclear groups (Del Sesto 1980), with the NRC and other governmental agencies and elected officials occupying a middle ground, some supporting and others opposing nuclear power. Two clearly delineated advocacy coalitions emerged. Sabatier (1988) notes that advocacy coalitions are differentiated by their commitment to a certain set of core values and beliefs that are generally unchanging, and that, unlike more peripheral values, cannot be compromised. In some domains, conflict revolves around beliefs that are fairly malleable, and then bargaining and compromise are possible. This is not so in the nuclear power domain. Del Sesto found that the nuclear power debate is not about the safety of nuclear plants, but rather is centered on "ideological differences about the nature and the appropriate direction of public policy" (1980, 40).

POLITICAL DYNAMICS OF NUCLEAR ACCIDENTS AS FOCUSING EVENTS

Nuclear power policy making is much more complex than in the oil spill, earthquake, or hurricane domains. There are a number of potential explanations for why nuclear power is so different from these other domains that also explain why focusing event politics in this domain differs substantially from the others studied here.

First, in contrast to the other three domains studied, the harms that may result from nuclear power generally, and accidents in particular, have thus far been invisible. They have been subject to debate, conflict, and differing interpretations. Unlike the other domains, the debate over the dangers of nuclear power centers on whether accidents like TMI or others are actually harmful, and if so, to what extent. In the United States, no life has demonstrably been lost as a direct result of civilian nuclear power generation. Thus, Thomas Dye (1992) has a sanguine attitude toward nuclear power, asserting that it is the safest and cleanest form of energy. He attributes the "meltdown" of the nuclear industry to political agitation by "no-nuke groups" rather than to the economics of nuclear power or safety issues surrounding the technology. TMI is dismissed as unimportant, and the debate in the scientific community over nuclear power is barely mentioned.

Dye may be overstating his case. Science was clearly at the heart of the controversy over nuclear power, as illustrated by the NRC's 1979 repudiation of the Rasmussen report. The Rasmussen study was initiated by the AEC and conducted in the mid-1970s by a prominent nuclear physicist. It argued that the engineered safety features in nuclear power plants made the risks of nuclear power accidents infinitesimally small. The Union of Concerned Scientists (UCS) strongly challenged the study on *scientific* grounds, refuting "its methodology and the very assumptions underlying the report. Fundamental disagreement among scientists persists, exacerbated by the potentially catastrophic nature of nuclear risk" (Nelkin 1981, 134). The controversy exists because "efforts to estimate the risks of an accident, or the severity of health hazards should one occur, are beset by technical uncertainties." Even the radiation assessments after the TMI accident were so variable that partisans in the scientific community and outside it could select data to buttress their claims" (Nelkin 1981, 134–35). With so much contention in the scientific community over whether and to what extent the TMI accident was "serious," it was clearly difficult to develop a national consensus that nuclear power is extremely dangerous. "The very language used to describe the [TMI] accident revealed the very diverse perceptions that enter such interpretations. Was it an accident or an incident? A catastrophe or a mishap? A disaster or an event? A technical failure or a simple mechanical breakdown?" (Nelkin 1981, 135).

This leads directly to nuclear power's second difference. In chapter 3 I argued that a major difference between earthquakes and hurricanes was the degree to which the risk of these disasters is dread. Dread risks are those risks about which people are most concerned, fearful, or anxious. Dread risks may lead to demands for government regulation of an industry or product out of proportion to the potential or actual harms resulting from the hazard. Dread is a function of, among other things, the level of knowledge of a hazard (the higher the knowledge, the lower the dread) and the potential for catastrophe involved with the hazard. With nuclear power, the level of dread is so great because the risks involved with the technology are so great and because lay understanding of the technology and its risks is rather limited. As Morgan (1993) notes, the most dread risks are not necessarily the most dangerous—arguably, bathtubs and bicycles are more dangerous than nuclear power plants. Yet the nuclear power industry has acknowledged that, even if a major accident has not yet happened, the potential for disaster from a major accident is great. For the nuclear power industry, this danger was once a source of pride and professional prestige. "Ironically . . . much of the reason for the shifting image of the nuclear power industry came from the almost perverse pride the leaders of the industry took in its early years in proclaiming that they were going to harness 'the world's most dangerous technology'" (Baumgartner and Jones 1993, 69).

In sum, nuclear power gained so much attention from citizens and groups because it was so exotic, dangerous, relatively hard to understand by the lay public, and inevitably confounded with its close technological and institutional relationship with nuclear weapons. Under these conditions, it is unsurprising that the politics of nuclear power are quite different from the politics of the better-understood, well-known hazards discussed in chapters 3 and 4.

Third, related to controversy over the risk of catastrophe (as exemplified by the heated debate over the Rasmussen Report), it must be remembered that nuclear power is still an immature technology; our experience with it and our reactions to it are still being formed. This point is often disputed by representatives of the nuclear power industry, who point out that the electric utilities have many hundreds of reactor-years' experience with running nuclear plants.[5] The industry's experience with operating particularly large power plants—greater than 1,000 megawatts electric (mWe)—is considerably more limited, closer to 30 reactor-years. This is relatively little experience, given the complexity of the technology and the potential, however slim, for disaster (Perrow 1984, 33). Even if the technical issues and the safety risks of nuclear power were well-established (and doubts persist on this count), the social systems necessary to manage such dangerous technology are less advanced than the technology itself. The Kemeny Commission, the body appointed by President Carter to investigate the TMI accident, "saw the TMI accident less as a technical than a social system failure that derived in part from the nature of social relationships among the leading actors in the nuclear enterprise" (Nelkin 1981, 141).

Fourth, nuclear power is very different because, unlike oil spills, earthquakes, and hurricanes, it is very difficult to identify accidents and to understand their relative severity when there are no immediate harms. Part of the problem involved in identifying nuclear power plant accidents or incidents is that, since they are generally not obviously injurious, they must be reported by utilities to the NRC, or the NRC must find out about a problem through its inspection process. Plants are required by law to report "abnormal occurrences" to the NRC, but the definition of abnormal occurrence is relatively vague and the incentives to report problems to NRC are, in some instances, less compelling than a utility's desire not to call attention to an accident.

This study uses the NRC AORs as the basis for the set of potential focusing events in this domain. I am confident that this is the best such compilation of events, as no accident mentioned by Congress between 1979 and 1990 fails to appear on the AOR list. Still, many of these events were relatively minor, and none of them can be said to have led directly to deaths or property damage. Thus, much more so than in the previous domains studied, the definition of a nuclear accident is as much an interpretive act as it is a matter of observation and reporting.

This has a substantial influence on nuclear policy making. In the nuclear power domain, there is a well-established, entrenched pair of opposing advocacy coalitions that hold their values deeply and pursue their preferences very actively. Events, even those as "big" (in subjective terms) as the TMI accident, are unlikely to substantially change their agendas or tactics. Given the difficulties involved with the interpretation of events (since a nuclear power plant accident is generally not self-evident), neither side has any incentive to seek to contain the event.

From the perspective of the antinuclear side, any accident is an exemplar of what can go wrong with a nuclear power plant and is a cause for concern, if not alarm. For the pronuclear advocates, no civilian nuclear power plant accident has demonstrably led to any deaths, nor has a consensus been reached on whether nuclear power plants have released injurious radiation during any incident. Thus, any "abnormal occurrence" or "event" stands as evidence that safety systems work, that the technology is manageable, and that the utilities are trustworthy and competent to manage the technology. The ambiguity of the harms and of the broader meaning of these accidents makes the events more susceptible to interpretation and debate, thus providing no incentive for pronuclear forces to contain the fact of the event.

This contrasts with the natural disaster domains, in which the physical damage of an event—flooding, landslides, and damaged or destroyed buildings—is clear even to the casual observer. A more interesting contrast is with another humanly caused disaster, oil spills. The obvious aesthetic harms that result from an oil spill are so overwhelming that they form excellent symbols that can be used or manipulated by antioil groups. There appears to be no positive interpretation that can be made of oil spills, only less negative ones, such as "the spill didn't do much damage because it evaporated quickly/sank quickly/wasn't really that much oil in the big scheme/ was out at sea and therefore harmed no coastal resources." This is a relatively weak and defensive response, compared with "the accident showed that safety systems worked." Oil companies are therefore much more prone to try to ignore and not play up oil spills, as reflected in the analysis in chapter 4. Since nuclear power plant accidents require far more interpretation by pro- and antiindustry forces, pro and antinuclear forces are roughly equally likely to cite particular events as evidence of the dangers of nuclear power or as evidence that existing systems work. In short, the tendency to wait for the problem to go away, in agenda terms, is far less pronounced in nuclear power than in oil spills.

To conclude this discussion, it seems clear that the identification of accidents—how harmful, how important, or even whether an accident occurred at all—is largely a process of social construction, not simply empirical observation and measurement. This stands in contrast to the earthquake, hurricane, and oil spill domains, where the fact of the event is fairly obvious to local citizens and, eventually, to national news media observers. Destroyed buildings and oily shorelines and beaches are, clearly, easier images to see, understand, and interpret. Even in the oil spill domain, where there continues to be considerable controversy over whether and to what extent oil spills damage the environment, most people still find large quantities of spilled oil disturbing, if only for aesthetic reasons. The nuclear accident, on the other hand, is very difficult to experience visually—there is no external evidence of the accidents considered in my database, nor was there any visible evidence of the other serious accidents in this domain that happened before my data set begins.

Policy Community Reaction to TMI

As expected, most observers argued that the TMI accident was a critical event in the history of nuclear power (Sylves 1980; Temples 1980). However, Baumgartner and Jones (1993) and Joppke (1993) note that the TMI accident did not significantly change the fortunes of nuclear power. Rather, the event simply intensified trends that had started in the early 1970s, the suspicions that nuclear power was economically uncompetitive with other energy sources and that it could not, under even the relatively less stringent regulatory strictures of the AEC era, compete with traditional sources of energy for electrical generation.

The TMI accident did lead, however, to an important mobilization opportunity for the antinuclear movement, culminating with the huge protest rallies held in New York and Washington to signal widespread opposition to nuclear power. But TMI, and all other events in this domain, cannot really be said to be focal in the same sense that events are focal in the other domains studied in this book. The empirical assessment of this claim is provided in Table 5-3. In chapter 3, I found that the earthquake and hurricane domains are predominantly event-driven. While the corresponding table in the oil spill discussion showed that there is an important intraevent community dealing with oil spills, other data suggest that particular events are also important in the oil spill domain. In this domain, however, we find that the vast bulk of testimony on nuclear power is offered not about particular events, but about nuclear power in general. Even when accidents occur, it is hard to suggest that this domain is particularly event-driven. In summary, the ambiguity of the events in the domain; the existence of two long-standing, highly visible, and contending advocacy coalitions; and the great extent to which the contending sides are polarized make focusing events far less powerful than those we have seen in the other domains.

The contending groups that were debating nuclear power were already highly polarized before the TMI event and the other events in the domain. Strongly pronuclear groups such as utilities, nuclear power trade associations, contractors, and the federal energy department were very strongly supportive of nuclear power, with a mean testimony tone of 0.456, while historically antinuclear groups overall had a testimony tone of −0.641. Individual groups that we would associate with

TABLE 5-3 Testimony, Field Hearings, and Testimony Centered on Events

Hearing Type		Centered on an Event	All Others	Total
Field	Mean tone[a]	0.000	−0.590	−0.557
	N	10	173	183
	Modal Policy[b]	Plant Safety	Licensing	Licensing
Washington	Mean tone	0.044	0.105	0.094
	N	226	981	1207
	Modal Policy	Cleanup	Licensing	Licensing
Total	Mean tone	0.042	0.001	0.008
	N	236	1154	1390
	Modal Policy	Cleanup	Licensing	Licensing

Notes:
For total analysis of variance on mean tone: $F_{3,1386}$ = 30.515, p = 0.000
For distribution of hearing type and testimony type, Chi-squared with 1 df = 19.821, $p<0.000$
[a]Tone is a measure of attitudes toward existing policy, where +1 indicates general support for existing policy, −1 indicates opposition to existing policy, and 0 is neutral.
[b]Policy type is the predominant topic discussed by the witness in a congressional hearing, based on the review of testimony in each domain.

the pro- and antinuclear positions show quite high tone values in the appropriate directions. With this degree of polarization already existing in the domain, it is unlikely that any one event will change the balance of political power in the long run. This is reflected in the overall tone of testimony in the domain, 0.008, or very close to neutral. The domain is polarized and deadlocked "in the middle," with neither position historically gaining the upper hand in this domain. TMI and other events, as shown in Table 5-3, seem to have little influence on this balance.

In addition, pronuclear partisans are not at all shy about mentioning TMI and other events in their testimony. The three groups most likely to mention a focusing event in their testimony were the NRC, privately owned nuclear utilities, and the nuclear power trade groups. This contrasts sharply with the oil spill case, in which environmental groups were most likely to mention and promote the event as an exemplar of policy failure, while oil companies and their allies sought to contain the event by ignoring it, mentioning it only when directly required to do so in a congressional hearing. In the polarized nuclear power domain, where events can be depicted as "accidents" on the one hand or "incidents" on the other, pronuclear advocates have little incentive to hide or ignore an event. They do, on the other hand, have a considerable interest in seeking to control the interpretation of the event and to contain that interpretation within a positive discourse, and they do so with alacrity.

Another aspect of nuclear politics revealed in this analysis is the extent to which the political coalitions and the terms of the debate had already been set before TMI or other events. The high degree of polarization, coupled with the extremely high levels of antinuclear activity without any direct reference to TMI, show that this domain is not primarily event-driven. I acknowledge that a witness's failure to directly mention TMI does not exclude the possibility that it might be mentioned, in passing, in the testimony. However, mentioning an event in passing can be a witness' off-hand comment, not a conscious effort to introduce the accident as an exemplar of what went right or wrong in the accident.

This reveals two features that are important for an understanding of nuclear agenda politics. First, it appears that when a nuclear power plant accident occurs, it is more likely to be elevated immediately to a national, not local, level of decision making. After all, the NRC, not the state environmental agencies, regulates nuclear power, and the debate is not simply between the local utility and local residents and intervenors, with the government mediating the dispute. Second, a nuclear power plant accident is likely to be seized upon immediately by large, nationally oriented pronuclear groups as a sign that the system of regulation is working and that engineered "defense in depth" systems work to contain accidents (the "progress frame" described by Gamson and Modigliani). Antinuclear groups will argue that the technology has gone beyond human abilities to contain accidents and therefore must be stopped. The nature of nuclear technology—expensive, exotic, dangerous, developed, regulated, and promoted by the federal government—expands any accident or incident immediately to among the most active and vocal participants in the domain, the pro- and antinuclear power advocacy coalitions.

Three Accidents, but Only One Focusing Event: Fermi, Browns Ferry, and TMI

Since the social construction of an event as an "incident" or "accident" is more important in this domain than in the others, it follows that similar events within the domain may have considerably different political outcomes and agenda effects. These outcomes are a function of relationships between events and the current political environment in which they occurred. If this is true, then nuclear power plant accidents that are similar in seriousness—that is, are similar in their potential for widespread harm—could yield considerably different agenda politics, depending on the nature of the participants in the debate and the nature of the political conflict in the domain. To illustrate these differences, I compare three of the most serious nuclear power plant accidents in United States history: the Enrico Fermi Nuclear Power Plant accident in Detroit in the fall of 1966, the Browns Ferry accident in Alabama in 1975, and the TMI accident in March 1979. In all three of these accidents, substantial harms could have resulted from radiation leaks from out-of-control reactors. Only the TMI accident gained widespread political attention. It is important to understand why.

The first of these accidents was the near-disastrous accident at the Enrico Fermi nuclear plant.[6] The plant, the only sodium-cooled breeder reactor placed in commercial service in the United States, was being readied for full-power operations. The possibility of disaster at the plant had been acknowledged by the Atomic Energy Commission. The AEC estimated that "given a severe accident at Fermi with unfavorable wind conditions, 133,000 people would receive high doses of radiation, and one-half would quickly die" (Perrow 1984, 50). Clearly, this would be a catastrophe on a scale never seen at one time and one place in the United States.

In this accident, the Fermi plant had a problem with its liquid sodium coolant. Under normal circumstances, problems with the coolant system would automatically "scram," or shut down, the reactor. This was not a normal circumstance, however; and the plant had to be manually scrammed[7] over several hours—a particularly difficult process, given the experimental nature of the coolant system. Once the reactor was no longer critical (meaning that there was no longer a meaningful atomic chain reaction in the fuel), "for a month the reactor sat there while the company let it cool off and planned the next step" (Perrow 1984, 52). The operators had to take extreme measures to ensure that radiation did not leak as the partially melted fuel was removed from the plant. Perrow notes that the fuel was placed into 9-foot-diameter, 18-ton cylinders that could withstand a 30-foot fall and a 30-minute fire. The reason for such precautions is dramatic: "Leakage from the casks could kill children a half a mile away" (Perrow 1984, 53). Three years passed before the materials were removed from the plant.

The Fermi plant incident is remarkable in two ways. First, it is remarkable in its seriousness (Gamson and Modigliani 1989, 14; Perrow 1984). Had the containment been breached because of overpressure or a partial core melt, deadly radiation could have killed or sickened tens of thousands of people. The risks were compounded by the fact that the plant was built near a heavily populated area, used particularly

deadly plutonium fuel, and was largely an experimental design. Ultimately, the plant was recommissioned for a time, but was then shut
down permanently.

Second, the Fermi accident was remarkable in the paucity of news
coverage and public attention it received. "More than five weeks after
the accident, the *New York Times* carried a story on what it labeled a
'mishap' at the Fermi nuclear reactor. There was nothing in the least
alarming in the *Times* account" (Gamson and Modigliani 1989, 14).
The reason for this blasé response was that "there was no significant
antinuclear-power discourse during this era," and therefore there were
no antinuclear activists to counter what Gamson and Modigliani call
the "progress package" of discourse on this issue. It was, as they note,
a nonevent because no one was available, or made available, to provide
an alternative story of the accident that would convey its seriousness.

The second serious event in this period was the 1975 accident at
the Browns Ferry nuclear power plant, operated by the Tennessee
Valley Authority (TVA). In the Browns Ferry accident, a technician
was inspecting cables, using a candle for illumination. Clarfield and
Weicek summarize the accident:

> TVA, which had become the world's foremost nuclear utility, operated
> twin 1,100 mWe [megawatt electric] reactors at Browns Ferry in northern
> Alabama. An electrician was checking for drafts by holding a candle near
> suspect sites, when a draft caught the flame and ignited some flammable
> insulation. The fire spread rapidly though the cable systems, requiring
> that both reactors be scrammed. It destroyed all five ECCS [Emergency
> Core Cooling Systems] of one of the units, knocked out 15 percent of
> capacity on the TVA grid and raised the electricity bills of TVA's customers
> for the cost of replacement electricity, which must often be bought off the
> national grid at premium prices (Clarfield and Weicek 1984, 377).

The possibility for catastrophe exists any time any portion of the
ECCS system is compromised, and the system was rendered safe only
through the efforts of technical personnel to find ways to run the
ECCS without the necessary connections between the controllers and
the reactors.

Yet again, this event attracted relatively little attention, even while
the antinuclear movement was gaining strength. The antinuclear movement propagated what Gamson and Modigliani call the "soft paths,"
"public accountability," and "not cost effective" packages of discourse
on nuclear power. These discourses were, however, subordinate to the
"progress" discourse which dominated media coverage and public
understandings of nuclear power, "even though its earlier hegemony
had been destroyed" (Gamson and Modigliani 1989, 15). While not

hegemonic, the progress story still held considerable sway over the public and press.

In neither of these cases was the news coverage or the political fallout nearly as evident as it was after TMI. Perrow notes that most accidents at nuclear plants would merit very little coverage except that they took place at a nuclear plant, and that, at any rate, the coverage of such events becomes more prevalent after TMI. The task at hand is to understand what made TMI different. TMI is different because of differences in the *political environment* between Fermi, Browns Ferry, and TMI.

There are at least two elements of the political environment that distinguish TMI from the Fermi and Browns Ferry accidents. The first of these elements is the existence of an active, visible, well-established antinuclear movement. By the time of the TMI accident, the antinuclear movement was firmly in place. The UCS, Critical Mass, national environmental groups, and local groups had formed networks and they had advanced and participated in the debate over nuclear power. These groups' efforts did not lead to the complete demise of nuclear power, but they helped to raise mass and elite consciousness of the dangers of nuclear power. These groups scored a considerable success by persuading Congress to dismantle the nuclear regulatory system that was established in the Atomic Energy Act. In so doing, the nuclear promotion function was divorced from the nuclear regulatory function, and the NRC was to take a more active role in regulating nuclear power for safety. The AORs that I use to track nuclear power plant accidents were an outgrowth of this increased safety concern from both the legislative and executive branches.

In addition, the Congress ensured that the nuclear power policy monopoly would be broken up when it abolished the Joint Committee on Atomic Energy and distributed congressional jurisdiction among several communities, most prominent of which in this study are the Senate and House Interior committees. Allowing more committees, with more open procedures, to participate in policy making was an invitation to venue shopping for both sides of the nuclear debate. The broadening of institutional avenues for interest group participation in nuclear power resulted in broadening of the scope of conflict. As Schattschneider (1960/1975) predicted, and as Baumgartner and Jones (1993) showed, increased scrutiny in this domain meant increased skepticism of the safety and economy of nuclear power, increased scrutiny of the nuclear power establishment generally, and increased visibility for antinuclear groups.

From the antinuclear perspective, serendipity also played a role. The film *The China Syndrome* was released in late 1978. This film depicted, in considerable technical detail, the kinds of events that could lead to a loss-of-coolant accident in a commercial nuclear reactor. The film was heralded by antinuclear advocates as an explanation of the sorts of fears that had been rising for years about nuclear power. The nuclear industry, for its part, ridiculed the film and its star, Jane Fonda (making unsubtle comparisons between her antinuclear activism and her sympathies during the Vietnam war). Still, "the China Syndrome"[8] entered the vocabulary as a term for a core meltdown, as well as a powerful symbol of the dangers of nuclear power.

The second element that differentiates TMI from other nuclear accidents is the existence of the NRC itself. Considerable debate still rages on whether the NRC serves to regulate or to promote nuclear power (or both simultaneously). However, it is clear that the NRC's safety mission, as codified by Congress when it established the NRC in 1973 and as reinforced in the Energy Reorganization Act of 1974, is far more important to the NRC than any safety imperative was to the AEC. Still, the NRC did not begin to actively pursue its safety mandate until the Carter Administration appointed more safety-conscious members to the NRC. In turn, the NRC quietly repudiated the Rasmussen report (Clarfield and Weicek 1984, 375), stating that it no longer could concur with the study's conclusions that nuclear plant accidents were unlikely. Clearly, a new era of nuclear regulation was underway. Perhaps the best example of this greater safety consciousness was the Abnormal Occurrence Reports, which are required by law and are on the public record. It seems inconceivable that the policy monopoly governed by AEC and the JCAE would have stood for such levels of openness and such clear invitations to scrutiny as are provided by public accountings of serious atomic accidents. The breakup of the policy monopoly in this domain led to greater interest in nuclear issues from outside forces and to greater demand for information.

CONCLUSIONS

In this chapter I find that the ambiguity of the events in the nuclear power domain; the existence of two long-standing, highly visible, and contending advocacy coalitions; and the great extent to which the contending sides are polarized make focusing events far less powerful than those we have seen in the other domains. While events do not seem to have the same influence on the agenda as they do in the earthquake, hurricane, and oil spill domains, the analysis here provides further support for two important elements of the theory of focusing events and agenda change.

First, I show in this chapter that the nature of the events in a domain does matter. In the nuclear power domain, there was only one large (in terms of perceived seriousness, not injury or damage) and several smaller, less focal, less important events, both in agenda terms and in their perceived importance on the part of disputants in the domain. This contrasts sharply with the variation in size and influence of events in the other domains. While in all four domains it is the exceptional event that gains the most attention, in the earthquake, hurricane, and oil spill domains smaller events are often also cited and discussed as examples of problems and of the need for solutions. In the nuclear domain, by contrast, small events are generally unknown, discussed mainly by technical experts, if at all, and have little to contribute to the policy debate.

The reason for this difference, as I have noted throughout this chapter, is that earthquakes, hurricanes, and oil spills need far less interpretation by participants than do nuclear power plant accidents. Nuclear power plant accidents are invisible, often undetectable, and often difficult to characterize as accidents at all. Rather than address whether incidents are accidents or mere events, the NRC lumps all serious events together as "abnormal occurrences." It is up to the partisans in the debate, not the NRC, to decide whether these are accidents, incidents, or something even less important.

A second element of the nature of events is the familiar natural/human causation dichotomy, but with a twist. In both the earthquake and hurricane domains, no claim is made that these events themselves can be prevented. Rather, policy makers focus on pre-event (as with earthquakes) and postevent (as in hurricanes) mitigation responses. A similar focus on postevent mitigation is evident after large oil spills, but, as befits a phenomenon that is generally considered to be under human control, the preevent agenda is dominated by issues of assigning liability for spills should they happen. Liability is, of course, not an issue in natural disaster policy, except perhaps when negligence leads to building failure.

In nuclear power, by contrast, blame-fixing, finger pointing, and arguments over risk and harms dominate discussion even when no event is on the agenda. When an event is on the agenda—and the only important event is the TMI accident—arguments over what happened and what it meant in policy terms are much more important in nuclear power than in the other domains, where the meaning of an event is usually clear and alternative stories, such as Union Oil's attempt to blame the Santa Barbara oil spill on "mother nature," are quickly dismissed as peripheral to the debate.

The second element of my theory that is confirmed here is the proposition that the nature of the policy community conditions the resulting agenda politics. Thus, agenda politics when policy making is dominated by professionals who focus on technical issues (earthquakes) looks considerably different from distributive, post hoc disaster relief policy (hurricanes). Both the oil spill and nuclear power domains contain two polarized, constantly contentious advocacy coalitions. But in the oil spill domain, where oil spills have a clear, immediate, and obvious negative connotation, environmental groups seize on events as a mobilization resource, while oil interests and their allies lay low until the initial shock and anger over the spill has faded. Oil companies tend to deal with oil spills as abstractions, while environmentalists tend to deal with oil spills as discrete events that carry particular symbolic meanings.

The mobilization effect of nuclear power plant accidents is limited for two basic reasons. First, there are so few accidents, providing little opportunity to mobilize or for groups to learn how to exploit events to mobilize existing and would-be members. Second, the nature and impact of the events cited by the NRC as "abnormal" and thus potentially dangerous is so ambiguous that pronuclear advocates are able to provide alternative stories after events (such as "safety systems work") that blunt the messages propagated by antinuclear groups. Thus, even though TMI led to huge antinuclear rallies, the accident only slightly accelerated the increase in public opposition to nuclear power. Other trends such as costs, waste disposal, and local opposition to nearby plants had more to do with the decline of the nuclear power industry than did TMI.

What leads to polarization in this domain, then, has less to do with events, of which only one serious one is cited here, and has more to do with disputes over the possibility of more serious events and the probable harms that may result. Events thus become fodder for the debate, but do not significantly change the underlying issues, the players, or the structure of the nuclear policy community. Thus, one can say that nuclear power is highly controversial and that the policy community is very contentious and polarized. However, based on the evidence I find, one can say that nuclear power policy, except in the aftermath of Three Mile Island, is driven by focusing events.

6

The Importance of Focusing Events in Policy Making

In this chapter I conclude by considering two final issues that help to explain the importance of focusing events in policy making. First, I consider the process by which focusing events can lead to actual policy change, not simply greater attention to the problem. After considering the mechanism through which policy change can occur, I discuss two types of focusing events that have not yet been considered in this study. Such events include, on the one hand, focusing events in domains where very few potential focusing events have occurred before, and, on the other hand, focusing events in domains where the particular event is quite common, but where important features of the event make particular events much more important in agenda terms. These different kinds of potential focusing events suggest that there is considerable room for more research on this phenomenon.

The results of the case studies suggest that focusing events can work as a catalyst for policy change by serving as signals of policy failure and opportunities for participants in policy making to "learn." This learning is facilitated by the opportunities for policy advocacy afforded by a focusing event. This discussion is framed by Sabatier's (1988) advocacy coalition framework of policy change and learning. In particular, focusing events provide the raw material for what Sabatier calls "policy-oriented learning." Focusing events also open up policy communities to greater scrutiny, and therefore, as found in Baumgartner and Jones's study of the collapse of policy monopolies, lead to changes in the configuration of participants in policy making and, sometimes, to policy change itself.

ADVOCACY, ANALYSIS, AND POLICY CHANGE

For some time, students of the policy process considered policy analysis to be an apolitical and technical activity that is divorced from normative assessments of policy. But while "policy analysts of the decisionist persuasion would like to project the image of technical, nonpartisan problem solvers who map out the alternatives open to the policy maker and evaluate their consequences by means of . . . objective means of analysis," Majone argues that "the policy analyst is a producer of policy arguments, more similar to a lawyer . . . than to an engineer or a scientist" (Majone 1989, 21). Viewed in this light, policy change can be viewed as a result of ongoing policy analysis in the service of advocacy. In this depiction of the policy process, focusing events provide a source of information to contenders in policy debates that they can use to press for policy change, or must respond to when other advocates use it to press for change. In particular, focusing events provide evidence of policy failure that can be added to analytic *and* advocacy arguments by proponents of policy change. The usefulness of focusing events in this process is clearer when we contrast the process of routine program analysis and evaluation with analysis and evaluation triggered by sudden, dramatic, and unexpected focusing events.

Most policy evaluation is planned and routine, occurring at fixed times throughout the lifetime of a program. For example, sunset provisions provide "triggers for evaluation and termination" (Peters 1993, 165). The yearly appropriations process provides opportunities for a critical review and reappraisal of programs incident to their being funded or cut back. Appropriations hearings are routine and, particularly in the case of smaller or noncontroversial programs, testimony delivered at these hearings often changes little from year to year.

In this routine analytical environment, defenders of the status quo have substantial advantages over those who seek policy change. It is well known that there are important structural impediments to policy change. These features—federalism, the separation of powers, and decentralized power in the Congress—can be exploited by defenders of existing policy, even when programs come under political pressure or fiscal scrutiny. These features also inhibit the expansion of the scope of policy, as they can be used by opponents to thwart expansion or additional funding. Claims for additional resources are usually accompanied by data indicating that the program in question is working well, and that with more resources the program could be extended to address additional needs. For example, advocates for educational programs such as Head Start argue that the program is working well, but that there are many more children who could benefit from the program if only more money were made available.

These claims must contend with opponents' arguments and, without any additional information being provided to proponents or opponents as to the need for expansion or contraction of a program, stasis or, at best, incremental change is likely to result. Routine opportunities for evaluation thus trigger the participation of important members of the policy community, particularly those associated with the competing advocacy coalitions. But this routine analysis will be treated in a routine way: the analyses will be subject to partisan scrutiny, which includes questioning the validity of the underlying data, challenging the methodology of the evaluation, and ultimately challenging the motives of the producers of this analysis.

Focusing events provide an opportunity for advocacy in the guise of analysis, but have substantial benefits for advocates of policy change. Focusing events are unplanned and unpredictable, and unpredictable events force all sides of a policy controversy to respond to a perception of policy failure, or at least a severe problem with existing policy, at the same time. Over the space of a few weeks or months, members of the dominant advocacy coalition—dominant because, presumably, they have greater resources available to promote their preferred solutions and prevent major change—may regain their analytical advocacy advantage. But the routine analytical and advocacy advantages of the dominant advocacy coalition may be overcome by the drama and graphic depiction of a problem, and of policy failure, symbolized by focusing events.

Indeed, focusing events, because they are so dramatic, sudden, and seemingly indicative of policy failure, can provide substantial benefits to advocates for policy change, particularly because focusing events usually indicate that something is going wrong, not that something is going well. Natural disasters, oil spills, and nuclear power plant accidents are generally bad news. They would, at least initially, support demands for policy change or, in the case of nuclear power, would support halting a policy of liberalizing licensing requirements. The advantage gained by focusing events can be attributed to the dramatic, symbolic, and visceral power of these events, which can overcome more technical or statistical policy analysis.

Many political scientists argue that policy analysis has problems that diminish its social scientific value. These include difficulties in gathering data (seen here in damage assessment after oil spills and nuclear power plant accidents), problems in measuring the actual effects or effectiveness of policy, and methodological problems, failures, and abuses, such as the misapplication of cost-benefit analysis (Anderson 1994, chapter 7; Dye 1992, chapter 14). These technical shortcomings of policy analysis recede in importance in the face of a dramatic focusing event and its use in policy argument. Focusing events do not gain their focal power from the accretion of evidence, but rather from their symbolic value. If analysts are engaged in advocacy, given that the goal of advocacy is to change policy, it is of little consequence whether the warrant for policy change is provided by outstanding analysis or by symbol-rich, emotionally charged events. Indeed, the advocate is best served by using the imagery surrounding events because it is far more likely to arouse public interest and support for policy change to ensure that "this does not happen again." This is not to say that the analyst needs to be intellectually dishonest, relying solely on dramatic events instead of more stringent analysis. But it does mean that the advocate who has plausible research results *and* a highly visible, tangible, and dramatic event on his or her side is likely to do better in a policy debate than an advocate with only evaluation data. This, in turn, can lead to more rapid nonincremental policy change in light of the event.

Focusing Events as Evidence of Policy Failure

Key to the argument of change advocates is the assertion that policy has in some way failed. Policy failure can take many forms: policy can fail to meet the goals set for itself, it can cost more than it was planned to cost, or it can create unintended effects on other populations. Advocates for change might argue that policy has failed because not enough money or other resources were committed to the program, or that the underlying causal theory contained in the policy is faulty. Whatever the reason, policy failure is not self-evident, but is itself the subject of intensive policy debate (Ingram and Mann 1980; May 1992).

It is difficult to demonstrate policy failure—and difficult to press for policy change—because once a program is created, it creates inertia that is very hard to overcome. Clients, targets, and beneficiaries of policy make difficult and costly adjustments to a new policy environment, and they prefer not to make further changes that open new issues of cost and benefit distribution (Peters 1993, 162). This entrenchment varies with the extent to which the policy community or issue network resembles an "iron triangle," in which case change is less likely, or a looser "issue network," where change may be somewhat more likely, provided that the appropriate impetus for change is present. As long as the most powerful members of the policy community continue to benefit from existing policy, entrenched interests will resist, usually successfully, any claims that policy has failed.

Focusing events can provide an impetus for change that overcomes inertia in a policy domain by providing dramatic evidence of some sort of policy failure, regardless of whether the claimed causal mechanisms are accurate. When an event occurs, the problem is very publicly and graphically highlighted so that an entirely new range of participants becomes involved. The result of increased scrutiny is rapid change in the policy community and greater potential for policy change.

These descriptions of policy change assume that policy change is generally opposed or at best viewed warily by members of the existing policy community. This is not always true; often, key members of the policy community support policy change, and the agency charged with administering a program may "volunteer" changes in policy (Peters 1993, 165). This is consistent with the internal mobilization style of agenda setting, where leading members of the policy community seek to mobilize greater public attention to a problem, in support of eventual policy change. As seen in the earthquake case, internal mobilization is most likely when there is only one advocacy coalition, dominated by expert policy makers, to advance ideas for change. If there are two or more advocacy coalitions, one coalition is likely to actively oppose the proposals of the other, as clearly reflected in the oil spill case.

Focusing events can therefore serve to trigger calls for policy change from inside or outside a policy community, depending on the style of policy making in that community and the alignment of political forces in the domain.

Policy Change and Learning

Some advocacy coalitions' goals are to change policy, while others seek to maintain the status quo. As argued throughout this book, prochange groups will often use focusing events to elevate issues on the agenda, with the policy change being the ultimate goal. In this section I specify one way of thinking about how focusing events can be used by groups to promote policy change. A particularly useful way of thinking about policy change is as the result of a learning process. Who learns, what is learned, and how learning is employed has been defined rather differently by a number of students of the policy process (Bennett and Howlett 1992). The main controversy in the debate over who learns is whether nonhuman entities such as institutions or organizations can "learn" or whether only individuals are the objects of learning. Sabatier (1988) and May (1992) deal with this problem by using individuals—agency heads, interest group leaders, academics, journalists, and so on—not institutions, as the unit of analysis in studies of policy making and learning. Such a definition of the subjects of learning is entirely consistent with the depiction of focusing events in this book as being events that influence the activities of individual actors in the policy process.

Sabatier provides a more specific definition of "policy-oriented learning" as "relatively enduring alterations of thought or behavioral intentions which result from experience and which are concerned with the attainment (or revision) of policy objectives" (Sabatier 1988, 133).

A focusing event can be an important contributor to policy-oriented learning, because events can clearly alter the thinking of members of the contending advocacy coalitions, leading to shifts in the balance of forces supporting or opposing policy change. Sabatier's definition, by concentrating on individual actors as members of advocacy coalitions, avoids attributing cognitive processes to organizations, while broadening policy making to include influential actors, such as academics and journalists, that institutionally based analyses tend to overlook. This focus on the individual as policy actor also overcomes the tendency to think of agencies or institutions as the objects of learning.

Types of Learning

The role of focusing events in policy-oriented learning differs with the different kind of learning that occurs in response to these events. May (1992) divides learning into three categories: instrumental policy learning, social policy learning, and political learning. In all three types of learning, policy failure—politically and socially defined—provides a stimulus for learning about how to make better policy. Failure might be considered as a consensus that a policy is failing to meet its goals, or is too costly relative to the goals that are attained. In a broader sense, failure can be the result of nonexistent policy in a particular area, which leads to attempts by some policy entrepreneurs to fill a policy vacuum. Whatever the nature of perceived failure, focusing events can serve to highlight failure and trigger calls for improved policy.

   Instrumental policy learning concerns learning about "viability of policy interventions or implementation designs." This sort of learning centers on implementation tools and techniques. If this learning is successful, policy is redesigned to take new information into account, thereby improving policy implementation. Social policy learning involves learning about the "social construction of a policy or program." This type of learning goes beyond simple adjustments to program management, and goes to the heart of the problem itself, including attitudes toward program goals and the nature and appropriateness of government action. If successfully applied, social policy learning can result in better understanding of the underlying causal mechanisms of a public problem, leading to better policy responses. Political learning, which may be the most prominent type of learning in the wake of focusing events, involves learning about "strategy for advocating a given policy idea or problem," leading potentially to "more sophisticated advocacy of a policy idea or problem."

   In the ideal case, learning reflects the accumulation and application of knowledge to lead to factually and logically correct conclusions.

However, policy makers and their supporters may support policy change that is not objectively related to change in the political environment or the nature of the problem. May calls mimicking or copying policy without assessment or analysis superstitious instrumental learning. Lotteries and tax policy to attract additional industrial development are sometimes examples of this sort of mimicking. For present purposes, however, it is enough to assume that a focusing event induces a response by participants in policy making, and, presumably, the more focal the event, the greater the response (in terms of group activity or agenda change) will be. This response is reflected in the increased levels of policy making manifested as increased attention to the problem on the congressional agenda.

The *Exxon Valdez* oil spill provides prima facie evidence of instrumental policy learning. Instrumental policy learning involves assessing the efficacy of existing policy instruments. Before the *Exxon Valdez* spill, a consensus had been reached (in part as a result of earlier oil spills) that oil spills were undesirable and that the federal government should in some way be involved in liability and cleanup schemes. No substantial disagreement existed on whether there should be federal policy to deal, in some way, with the oil spill problem. But by 1989, federal oil spill policy was disjointed, with no less than three separate funds established to defray the costs of oil spill response and cleanup. Liability limits were relatively low, and no clear lines of responsibility were established to ensure an appropriate response to large oil spills. The *Exxon Valdez* spill was used by environmental groups and their allies to argue, much more strongly than had been possible before the spill, that these policy tools failed to address large oil spills. The resulting legislation, the Oil Pollution Act of 1990, combined the separate spill funds into one large federal fund, increased liability limits, and specified clearer lines of authority to improve response to spills. The Oil Pollution Act was a significant change in the *instruments* with which the federal government sought to prevent oil spills and to clean up those that occur, even though the goals were largely identical to those that existed before the *Exxon Valdez* spill.

Evidence of social policy learning—such as change in the social construction of problems—appears in the debates that led to the enactment of the National Flood Insurance Program (NFIP) in 1973 and the National Earthquake Hazards Reduction Act (NEHRA) of 1977. Social policy learning involves learning about the causal mechanisms that lead to problems. This learning can involve new understandings of these causal mechanisms, or learning about new and more effective ways in which these problems can be depicted to make advocacy more successful. Before the NFIP and the NEHRA, the primary goal of federal disaster policy, across all types of disasters, was postdisaster relief. Except for federal flood control programs, which combined elements of disaster mitigation with a healthy degree of distributive federal spending on local construction projects, the federal government had largely left disaster mitigation duties to state and local officials, through a decentralized process centered on state and local building codes. A series of disasters in the 1960s and early 1970s caused members of the disaster policy community, and the earthquake community in particular, to consider how federal policy might be reoriented toward mitigating disasters rather than simply responding to them after the fact. Central to this shift was the understanding that while we cannot predict many disasters nor prevent them from happening, we can alter our behaviors before events occur to make them less damaging. The construction of natural disasters as events for which preparations can be made to minimize injury and damage, rather than inevitable acts of God, shifted the nature of the debate and led to new policy such as the NEHRA.

Political learning involves learning about effective political advocacy. Political learning can be assumed to have occurred when advocates for or against policy change alter their strategy and tactics to conform with new information that has entered the political system. Of course, lessons can be learned well or learned poorly. In the aftermath of the Santa Barbara oil spill, the Union Oil company embarked on an aggressive campaign to argue that the spill was an act of God and was therefore not the fault of the oil company. This campaign failed in the face of local anger and, ultimately, evidence that it was technical failure, not "nature," that led to the well blowout. The lessons of this response seem to have been learned by the Exxon Company, which, in congressional hearings, took a much lower-key approach to issue containment. When Exxon did seek to fix blame for the spill, they cited a number of potential causes: the allegedly drunk captain, the unlicensed third mate at the helm, and even the ice floes that caused the tanker to deviate from the normal shipping lane. But Exxon was never as aggressive in its defense of its behavior as was Union Oil. This quiet strategy, however, was no more successful than Union's more aggressive strategy. Exxon's reticence was viewed by many as indifference and was widely castigated by environmentalists, elected officials, and local residents. If there was a political lesson to be learned here, Exxon did not quickly learn it.

Meanwhile, environmental groups seem to have learned from *Exxon Valdez* and similar events that these are excellent opportunities for member mobilization, membership drives, and fund-raising. Most major mainstream environmental organizations, such as the Friends of the Earth and the Sierra Club, used the *Exxon Valdez* spill as the centerpiece of mass mail campaigns to gain members and to induce existing members to donate funds and write and phone elected officials. Perhaps most importantly here, these groups used these events as opportunities to gain a place on the congressional agenda. They used this opportunity to invoke images of recent environmental catastrophes and to press for more stringent policy to prevent, it is hoped, future disasters.

Political learning was also evident in the efforts of antinuclear forces, even before the Three Mile Island accident. Local residents near existing or proposed nuclear plants formed intervenor groups to oppose licensing or impose tougher restrictions on nuclear plant operations. At the national level, the Union of Concerned Scientists was formed to provide a counterweight to the significant advocacy and analytic advantages held at the time by the nuclear industry. When the Three Mile Island accident occurred, these forces were in place to exploit it as a symbol of the problems of nuclear power. I argue that TMI did not lead to the demise of the nuclear industry; nevertheless, groups opposed to nuclear power used TMI as an example of the problems plaguing the industry and successfully prevented the relaxation of licensing rules for these plants. Group leaders learned that events like TMI and images like the specter of the "China Syndrome" were highly effective in promoting public and elite concerns about the safety and cost-effectiveness of nuclear power.

In sum, focusing events are an important part of the learning process for advocates of more aggressive policy to deal with earthquakes, oil spills, and nuclear power plant accidents. However, learning at the federal level is much less evident in the hurricane domain. This is due in large part to the failure of the hurricane policy community to evolve into an advocacy coalition parallel to that found in the earthquake domain. Such structures are necessary for this sort of learning and effective advocacy to occur.

The Necessity of Advocacy Coalitions for Policy Change

In the oil spill and earthquake domains, at least one important event played a role in eventual policy changes. In the nuclear power domain, one event—the Three Mile Island accident—derailed policy change designed to liberalize plant licensing procedures. But in the hurricane domain there is no evidence of meaningful change in federal policy toward these hazards as a result of a focusing event, suggesting that domains in which the agenda is seemingly event-driven do not necessarily experience event-related policy change. Rather, events merely provide a window of opportunity, in Kingdon's terms, in which the possibility of policy change is greater but far from certain. Any efforts to change policy must be led by advocacy coalition leaders who connect the event, as evidence of the problem, with potential solutions that are feasible in the existing political climate. In the hurricane domain, we need not even ask whether the political climate is favorable or whether solutions to the hurricane problem are available. Even if both conditions are met, there appear to be few, if any, advocates available to drive policy change in this domain, and policy stasis is the result. In short, while there may be a hurricane policy community, there is no hurricane advocacy coalition that has formed to use events as learning opportunities to advance new policy. Thus, much as an advocacy coalition must exist to react to a focusing event and advance it on the agenda, an advocacy coalition must also exist so that its members can learn about how current policy is or is not successful. Members of the coalition can then learn how to effectively propose new and more effective policy responses. Until such an advocacy coalition forms in the hurricane domain, there is little reason to believe that hurricanes will do more than elevate problems of disaster relief on the agenda, and then only very briefly.

The earthquake domain differs from the hurricane domain because the former contains an active advocacy coalition that promotes government response to earthquakes. The efforts of this coalition led to the passage of the National Earthquake Hazards Reduction Act (NEHRA) of 1977. The passage of the NEHRA was the result of a number of factors. But while these factors—an active scientific community, an entrepreneurial Senator, and a supportive science advisor—were all important elements of what Kingdon calls the policy "primordial soup," some sort of spark is needed give the primordial soup form and substance. That spark was the San Fernando earthquake, which, in conjunction with other factors, began a process that led to the enactment of the NEHRA. The difference between the earthquake and hurricane domains is that even when focusing events are present—hurricanes Camille and Agnes, for example—the primordial soup is too thin for the event to have much effect. The result is that policy making will be highly unlikely as long as no policy community exists to connect various elements of the policy problem and link them to potential solutions. In short, at least the beginnings of an active advocacy community are necessary ingredients of the policy primordial soup.

Even when there is an advocacy coalition available to advance policy ideas, policy making can be difficult. Internal mobilization requires that the most expert and active participants in the domain persuade citizens and their elected officials to support policy making when the payoffs from such policy may be difficult to understand. In the earthquake domain, the graphic destruction exemplified by the San Fernando earthquake and other earthquakes, and the potential for even greater disaster, coupled with the relatively small amounts of money involved in the NEHRA compared with the entire federal budget, made policy change rather more easily attained.

While the primordial soup may have been just right for policy change in the earthquake domain, the paradox in the oil spill and nuclear power domains is that the policy soup may not be "as primordial" as in the earthquake domain. Patterns of interest-group power, interaction, and conflict in the oil spill and nuclear power domains are relatively fixed and well known to all participants. In such cases, it may take particularly large events to overcome the dominant advocacy coalition's advantages and trigger policy change. This is the case in the oil spill domain. From the grounding of the *Argo Merchant* off Nantucket in 1976 to the massive *Exxon Valdez* oil spill in 1979, Congress had failed to pass comprehensive oil spill liability and prevention legislation that took state and federal interests into account. Congress had begun such an effort before the *Argo Merchant* grounding, but even that event failed to overcome major differences between the House of Representatives and the Senate. The main differences that divided the two chambers was the question of preemption by federal law of state liability laws. No event or political shift changed this deadlock; indeed, President Reagan's hostility to environmental regulation contributed to making this impasse even more difficult to resolve.

This deadlock remained in place until the *Exxon Valdez* spill. Observers and participants on both sides of the broader dispute agreed that this spill was the turning point in oil spill policy. After *Exxon Valdez*, oil companies initially sought an issue containment strategy that failed due to the size and extent of the spill. They then shifted to a political damage control strategy to limit the scope and costs of what seemed to be the inevitable legislative response to the *Exxon Valdez* spill. This was relatively more successful. The passage of the Oil Pollution Act (OPA) of 1990 was a loss for oil companies because it did not provide for federal preemption of state oil pollution liability laws. But it was also a partial victory for oil companies because it combined several federal spill cleanup funds, provided for an expanded Coast Guard role in spill response, and did not immediately require double-hulled oil tankers. Like much legislation, the OPA was a compromise.

For present purposes, the important lesson is that this legislation is so closely associated with a major event in the study, the *Exxon Valdez* spill. Where political conflict leads to a deadlock in policy making, it appears that only truly exceptional events that lead to considerable public and elite anger can sufficiently tip the balance to lead to policy change. Such a determination of exceptionality is often only possible on a post hoc basis. Regardless, the result is that policy change in a domain with two competing advocacy coalitions is very difficult, and focusing events come into play mainly when they are very large and are highly visible, so that they can be experienced at least vicariously and viscerally by a broad spectrum of the population. Under such conditions, mobilization through events is relatively easier than in the internal mobilization model exemplified by the earthquake case. The *Exxon Valdez* spill led to a public outcry, at least for a while, against oil spills and in favor of policies that would prevent future spills and punish careless spillers. This mobilization gave the prochange forces the strength to press for policy change and overcome the deadlock.

Patterns of group interaction are similar in the nuclear domain, even though the outcomes are quite different. There is only one truly important nuclear power plant event that had an influence on policy: the Three Mile Island accident. Since the agenda effects of all other events are tenuous at best, it is difficult to argue that smaller events had a discernible policy effect. But it is also difficult to assign to TMI a substantial influence on broader legislative policy. Focusing events thus can block and reverse trends toward policy change, as in nuclear power policy in the late 1970s. This blocking effect is the result of a change in roles of the resource-rich and the resource-poorer advocacy coalitions. In nuclear power the roles were reversed. By the late 1970s it was becoming clear that, under current regulations, the civilian nuclear power industry was unlikely to remain economically viable. Well before TMI, costs began to escalate and orders for new nuclear plants declined precipitously. These conditions were due in part to antinuclear activism, and in part to the unfavorable economics of generating electricity with a dangerous and exotic technology. Whatever the reason, the nuclear industry sought regulatory relief; in particular, it was seeking relaxed rules on nuclear plant licensing. Prospects for relaxed policy were good, as former nuclear engineer Jimmy Carter pressed for change. Factors favorable to change were the moribund state of the nuclear industry and the national response to the energy price shocks of the late 1970s, corresponding with the Iranian revolution, and leading again to concern about dependency on foreign oil.

This trend away from stringent regulation was derailed in large part by the TMI accident. In chapter 5 I argued that one cannot attribute the collapse of the civilian nuclear power market to the TMI accident; the trends that led to the downfall of this industry started well before TMI. But clearly the climate of fear and anger generated by the TMI accident made it virtually impossible for licensing reform to pass the Congress.

All this occurred as a result of an event that was quite intangible compared to the other events studied. TMI has not been demonstrated to kill anyone, no property was damaged, no wildlife habitat was ruined, and, indeed, one could stand outside the TMI plant during the accident and not really understand precisely what was wrong. The debate after the TMI accident turned on whether there really had been an "accident" at all. Antinuclear activists insisted on calling the event an accident. The event was so hard to quantify as a harm that nuclear power partisans could characterize the event as an "incident." They went further to argue that, while human and mechanical failures do happen in complex systems, TMI's safety systems worked (and other plants' systems would have worked the same way), and that there was no threat to human life. It would have been exceedingly difficult for Exxon to characterize the *Exxon Valdez* spill as an "incident," given the large volume of oil visibly spilled, while such a characterization was viable in the wake of TMI.

The debate over the meaning of TMI thus turned on the depiction of the event as "incident" or "accident." Meanwhile, although the event did lead to greater government and industry efforts to improve and tighten safety rules and systems in nuclear power plants, the accident cannot be said to have significantly affected the trend away from nuclear power in the United States; it was on the way down, and it continued to go down at about the same rate. Had the event not happened, it is possible, however, that some measure of regulatory relief may have been granted to the nuclear power industry.

Summary

Certainly, the process of policy change is complex, and a deterministic model of policy change may be impossible to design. Such a model would likely leave out a considerable degree of the nuance and contingency that characterizes any sort of policy making. The depiction of policy change in this chapter avoids determinism by suggesting that focusing events are sometimes a part of the "primordial soup" that precedes policy change. Indeed, focusing events may be a spark that helps make the primordial soup "thicker," leading, eventually, to policy change. Part of this soup is the existence of at least one advocacy coalition, a necessary, but not sufficient, condition for policy change. The mechanism for policy change—learning—relies on the interpretation of events by key members of advocacy coalitions. Without them, policy change is unlikely.

OTHER TYPES OF FOCUSING EVENTS

Clearly, beyond the four policy problems studied in this book, there are many other policy problems that might be illuminated by potentially focal events. In many of these domains, large events happen only once—the event appears to be focal because greater attention is paid by government and media to the problem, but it is difficult to detect patterns because there are no other such events in the domain. No one would deny, for example, that the space shuttle *Challenger* accident was a very focal event—news of the event dominated the following week's news, debate ensued for months over perceived failures at NASA and its contractors, and lay people and experts agonized over the costs and rewards of risking human lives to travel in space. Design features of the solid rocket boosters (primarily the well-known O-rings) were changed, and NASA launch guidelines were changed to prevent launches in the weather that is believed to have caused the O-ring failure. Other unique or extremely rare events include, to date, the two Tylenol poisoning incidents in the 1980s and the terrorist bombings of the World Trade Center and the Federal Building in Oklahoma City. In both these types of events, only a few incidents have occurred, making each event unique or near-unique.

It is impossible to assess the focal power of these events in the way I consider natural disasters and industrial accidents for two reasons. First, we cannot understand its influence on policy making over a substantial length of time. As Baumgartner and Jones might argue, by focusing on one-shot events we look at the punctuation, but not at the equilibrium. Second, we need several events to understand how events are similar and different from each other, particularly if we wish to model the relationship between focal attributes and efforts to set the agenda. In sum, if the theory of focusing events based on quantitative analysis is to be extended, it should be extended to domains in which a reasonable number of important events occur in the period of study. This is the implicit assumption made in selecting the domains in this study. To study events such as the *Challenger* disaster and the Oklahoma City bombing would require a more qualitative approach than that taken in this study. Still, the policy domain attributes introduced in chapter 2—domain organization, problem visibility, and public participation in policy making—will be important in understanding these events, much as they were important in understanding the events studied here.

Given these characteristics, it is possible to create three categories of focusing events, one of which I study here and two of which are not considered in this study. The type of category in which an event falls strongly suggests the method a researcher would use to understand how an event became focal.

The first category of events are what I call "normal" focusing events. These events are not "normal" in the sense that they are regular or routine. Rather, I use the term "normal" the same way Perrow (1984) uses the term: as an event that can be expected to happen sometime, given the complexity of technology or our propensity to live and work in risky areas. By this definition, earthquakes, hurricanes, oil spills, and nuclear plant accidents can be expected to happen eventually, even if they cannot be predicted. These events occur sufficiently often to allow us to isolate events and model their influence on the agenda.

The second type might be called "new" focusing events. A new focusing event is an event that has never happened before, or, if it has, happened so long ago as to have faded from memory. New focusing events happen because of changes in technology and changes in society. Three examples of new focusing events are the Tylenol poisoning incident in the early 1980s, the loss of the space shuttle *Challenger* in 1986, and the terrorist bombing of the Alfred P. Murrah Federal Building in Oklahoma City, Oklahoma, in 1995. All these events were novel or near-novel. The shuttle accident was novel for the simple reason that before 1981 the shuttle did not exist. If we extend our time horizon to the beginning of the space program, the technology had existed only 35 years before the loss of life in an American space vehicle in flight. Indeed, in only two accidents have astronauts lost their lives in spacecraft: the 1967 Apollo fire and the *Challenger* accident. There has been only one near-miss, the 1970 Apollo 13 mission. In the future there may very well be more accidents involving spacecraft, but the *Challenger* accident was the first involving an American spacecraft in flight. Because it was first accident of its kind, and because one of its passengers was Christa McAuliffe (also a unique feature of this flight), it attracted greater attention than, for example, a plane crash involving NASA or military personnel. Indeed, the loss of the *Challenger* is often characterized as a disaster; the images of the craft exploding in flight, and of the solid rocket boosters separating and careening wildly from the explosion are still indelibly etched in the minds of those who watched the launch, or replays of it, on national television. The accident grounded other shuttles for over two years as it was very carefully investigated and the cause isolated.

The accident led to the predictable search for blame that characterizes focusing events. In the end, there appears to be plenty to go around. It is well understood that the failure of the O-rings on one of the solid rocket boosters allowed hot gases to leak, igniting the large liquid fuel tank to which the shuttle is mated, thereby triggering an explosion.

But why did the O-ring fail? Various explanations have been offered, but from a political perspective this is not the most interesting part of the story. Rather, the ultimate importance of the *Challenger* accident (characterized by many in public service and the media as a "disaster") was the soul-searching among many Americans, and among NASA officials, that the event generated. This reexamination of American space policy was made simpler by the fact that the United States had already demonstrated its technical superiority over the Soviet Union by safely landing more than one person on the moon. By the mid-1980s, spaceflight was viewed by many as at best a routine act and at worst a quest for adventure that cost a great deal of money, put human lives at risk, and afforded little scientific payoff that could not be achieved through unmanned spaceflight.[1] After the *Challenger* accident, the danger became a much more prominent element of debates over spaceflight.

The Tylenol incidents were "new" because, while minor examples of product tampering had occurred before the Tylenol case, there had been no nationwide scare over the safety of such a ubiquitous consumer product. The scale of the problem was huge: Johnson & Johnson, parent of the company that makes Tylenol, stood to lose hundreds of millions of dollars and hard-won market share if the public had lost confidence in the product. Case studies of Johnson & Johnson's response to the Tylenol tampering incidents have become a staple of business school management classes. The firm has been widely praised for its effective and forthright handling of this tragedy, as it spent millions to rid the shelves of potentially dangerous products and then developed industry-standard packaging methods to make consumer products less prone to tampering. In this case, then, the Tylenol case was clearly focal; the problem gained widespread attention and actual policy change, such as a mandate for new packaging practices, was the result. The Tylenol case thus stands in stark contrast to the halting, bumbling response Exxon made to the *Exxon Valdez* spill.

The Oklahoma City bombing is novel because, while there had been terrorist incidents on United States soil before this bombing—most notably, the bombing of the World Trade Center in New York City in 1993—no such terrorist attack had, in living memory, killed so many people or done so much property damage in one place in the United States. Contributing to the novelty of the event was the government's apprehension of two American citizens allegedly associated with an increasing antigovernment sentiment that was becoming more violent. While the ultimate outcome of the investigation and trial is not known at this writing, the bombing was focal on several levels: it increased attention to the issue of terrorism in the United States, and it increased, if for a short time, media and government scrutiny of the antigovernment "militias" that had become more active in the early 1990s. Prima facie evidence of the focal importance of this event was the introduction of antiterrorism legislation after the bombing and the imposition of greater security measures at government office buildings nationwide.

I call the third type of focusing event "common events under uncommon circumstances." Such events are generally common events, such as accidents, that gain greater attention due to some unique and unusual feature of the event that makes them newsworthy and, not coincidentally, worthy of greater government attention and potential policy change. As this is being written, one such event came rather quickly into the national consciousness: the death of a seven-year-old girl attempting to set a "record" (not recognized by any sanctioning body) as the youngest "pilot" to fly across the United States. The crash of an individual single-engine private plane is an unremarkable event, and few, if any, of these crashes gain much attention because the circumstances in which they occurred are routine. The death of a seven-year-old child piloting a plane raises considerably more issues and questions than does a routine airplane crash. In the aftermath of this wreck the public and elected officials have raised questions involving FAA rules on who may manipulate flight controls under what circumstances. In the editorial pages and on talk shows, some members of the public have questioned the judgment of parents who would let their child attempt such a record, and questioned the judgment of the flight instructor in allowing the plane to take off in a storm.

Other "common" events include political scandals and violent crimes. Most would-be scandals never receive great public attention until something unique about the scandal attracts wider attention. Thus, President and Mrs. Clinton's involvement in the Whitewater land deal in Arkansas and Newt Gingrich's ethical problems have so far failed to grab as much attention as partisans in these issues may have hoped. This is because many Americans perceive these activities as "business as usual," either out of cynicism or a belief that such activities are simply a necessary part of politics. Scandals therefore need a unique and bizarre feature to gain broader attention, such as the revelation of taped Oval Office conversations in the Watergate affair or the diversion of funds from clandestine sales of arms to Iran to the Nicaraguan *contras* in the Iran-Contra affair.

Similarly, violent crimes are common events in the United States and are primarily local problems addressed by state and local authorities. But such events can become potential focusing events under appropriate conditions. Thus, the murder of Polly Klaas in California gained national attention due to particular features of the case, including the parents' active collaboration with the media to help find their daughter and the particularly brutal nature of Polly's abduction and murder. Later, the family was active in using the media as its means of pressing for severe punishment of the girl's murderer. Many families, when confronted with this sort of tragedy, seek to protect their privacy, and the memory of their loved ones, by avoiding extensive media exposure. The opposite occurred in the Klaas case, making this a unique and at least potentially a focusing event.

In summary, the focal power of new focusing events, or of common events under uncommon circumstances, derives from the unique characteristics of these events. What makes the event unique, and therefore focal, may best be described through qualitative study. The study of what makes these events focal must be more consciously historical and must track the activities of participants in the ensuing debate after each of these events. While these events are likely to be quite different from normal focusing events, the dynamics of the postevent political debate will likely be very similar to the process outlined in this book. The process includes claims of policy failure and the use of these events as evidence of policy failure and a warrant for change. Evidence of such processes is clear: the Oklahoma City bombing led to the passage, a year later, of antiterrorism legislation, and the girl pilot's death has led to a searching review of FAA rules concerning who may fly airplanes under particular conditions. The process by which these policies were made is unique to each case, however, and is deserving of further historical analysis.

CONCLUSION

Since Schattschneider's *The Semi-Sovereign People*, social scientists have known that the struggle to broaden or narrow the scope of political conflict is central to efforts to gain and hold political power. Such efforts include expanding or restricting the numbers of people who are aware of a problem and demand that something be done about it. However, as has been seen throughout this study, not all political conflict can be described as competition between two contending advocacy coalitions. The nature of policy making in any substantive area influences and is influenced by the style of agenda-building practiced by participants in the domain. The hurricane domain contains no discernible advocacy coalition, which results in a style of distributive policy that simply distributes federal largess after a disaster. Earthquakes provide an opportunity for earthquake professionals to expand an issue beyond the rather small group of policy entrepreneurs and legislative specialists who deal with earthquakes, and perhaps to provide a lesson for those who are concerned with hurricane policy.

Large oil spills and the controversy surrounding them are very difficult to contain, but oil companies and their allies seek to put their spin on spills and to counter the negative images propagated by environmental groups. The same patterns are reflected in nuclear power, except that nuclear power accidents are much less visible and tangible, and are therefore considerably easier to contain.

This is a classic pattern of interaction between less powerful and more powerful groups in society, where the less powerful seek to expand conflict and the more powerful seek to contain it. The classic way to contain conflict, of course, is to keep it off the agenda, "out of sight and out of mind." But some events and the stories surrounding them are ambiguous, and ignoring them, even in the name of issue containment, can be counterproductive. This is true in the nuclear power domain, where the remnants of the old nuclear policy monopoly do not seek to avoid discussing events to the same extent as prooil partisans after oil spills.

Focusing events are an important part of the agenda-setting and policy-making process. That this is true seems intuitive and obvious. Nearly any citizen who is involved in a particular issue or question can cite events that served as turning points in the progress of a proposal from inception to enactment. Focusing events often serve as those turning points. The participants in the congressional hearings I cite in this study often cited the San Fernando earthquake, the *Exxon Valdez* oil spill, or the Three Mile Island nuclear accident as "turning points" that provided "windows of opportunity" for greater attention to a problem and subsequent policy change.

This study goes beyond intuition to more systematically understand what factors lead to greater attention to public problems. The results show that, as in many of our studies of politics, the mechanisms by which focusing events influence politics are rather more complex, subtle, and contingent than intuition would suggest. For example, as students of the democratic process we might believe that an event that influences a great number of people would place greater pressure on elected officials to do something about a problem, compared with an event with an influence on fewer people. I find this not to be the case; the sheer scope of an event is not a determinant of the postevent institutional agenda. This should provide some comfort for those who believe that government should not respond to problems simply because large numbers of people (i.e., voters or taxpayers) are affected. But this is also a puzzle, because it leads to the important normative question of what should drive attention to a problem. Damage or the seriousness of the accident or disaster seems to be the important determinant of attention, suggesting that Congress does not randomly focus on problems but, rather, does focus on the more serious problems when their seriousness has been revealed by focusing events and when the seriousness of the event is widely agreed-upon.

The differences revealed in this study also show that focusing events, as broadly defined at the outset, do not behave the same way in all domains. The differences in the agenda-setting power of focusing events derives from the nature of the events themselves (natural versus humanly caused, level of dread) and the composition of the policy community that leads policy making in the domain (number of advocacy coalitions, types of participants). While the four domains studied here constitute a small set of the possible domains that are subject to focusing-event politics, progress has been made in understanding how the nature of the domain interacts with the characteristics of the event to result in a particular type of focusing-event politics. My hope is that future studies of this phenomenon will extend to other domains and levels of government to build on the findings and ideas developed here, and will provide a better developed sense of the ways in which focusing events move governmental agendas.

APPENDIX

Comments on the Method

In the models discussed in this book, the dependent variables are measures of congressional and news media agenda *activity*. I will discuss the construction of this variable. The independent variables listed in Table A-3 are derived from publicly available data on population, damage, event seriousness, and the like. The Testimony Database is the database constructed by reading and coding hearings in the respective policy domains. Congressional hearings were isolated by using the Congressional Information Service (CIS) CD-ROM database. All hearings are coded in a domain for the period under study, except for routine appropriations hearings, which are not included because they are regularly scheduled events in the budget cycle that change very little from year to year. The earthquake and hurricane data sets include data on events that occurred from 1960 to 1990, so the actual span of the data is from 1958, at the earliest, to 1992 at the latest. This allows us to capture preevent as well as postevent activity. The oil spill database contains events from 1968 to 1990, and the nuclear power database includes events from 1977 to 1990.

In the news activity analysis, zero-order correlation coefficients are used to allow for comparisons of the sign and magnitude of the variables, while the adjusted R^2 of the regression model is provided to assess the overall variance explained by the variables taken together. I also show the congressional agenda models using the same variables for comparative purposes. The congressional activity models are ordinary least squares (OLS) regression models. Any transformations made to variables to meet the assumptions of OLS regression (in particular, near-normally distributed variables) are indicated in Table A-3.

COMMENT ON THE AGENDA DENSITY VARIABLE

In chapter 2 I theorize that agenda activity (both institutional and media) is a function of a number of factors, grouped together in event attribute and political models. In understanding focusing events, the important issue in modeling agenda dynamics is the difference between agenda change and agenda density. Agenda change is the extent to which the institutional and news agendas grow or shrink in the two years after an event. Agenda density measures the extent to which an event dominates the agenda, regardless of agenda change. Density is measured by counting how much testimony was offered or how many news stories were published about a particular event in the two years following the event compared to the rest of the domain.

We might suppose that agenda change correlates with agenda density, since it seems sensible that truly focal events will both increase the size of the agenda and will dominate the agenda. This is borne out in the relationship between institutional agenda change and institutional agenda density, with change and density correlating at r = 0.409 and r = 0.404 for the earthquake and hurricane domains, respectively. This is not borne out in the media models, however, with media change and density correlating at r = 0.169 for the earthquake domain and r = −0.437 for the hurricane domain. In the hurricane domain this is clearly opposite of what is expected.

The reason for this anomaly in the media agenda is the way hurricanes bunch together. Hurricanes occur during a particular season, generally August through December, although sometimes earlier or later. When two or more events occur close together in time, one event is quite likely to dominate all others on the agenda, but the agenda change value for each event will be similar. An extreme example of this effect is demonstrated in Table A-1. Within the three-year period illustrated there were four events. The event with the greatest news density was Hurricane Gloria. This is unsurprising, as Gloria struck along the East Coast from Virginia to New England and did considerable damage on Long Island. Since the *New York Times* is used as the measure of media activity, this event gained considerably more attention as a local news story than the other events. This is true of a number of hurricanes that struck the Northeast. Hurricane Elena, as the first storm of the season, shows the greatest news agenda change, in spite of accounting for a low news density score. Hurricanes Juan and Kate failed to expand the news agenda beyond Elena's influence, so news change is negative in this period, while they did gain enough attention to be mentioned in approximately 19 percent and 29 percent, respectively, of stories about hurricanes in the study period. Thus, we see that a high level of news change in Hurricane Elena corresponds to a low news density score (the lowest in this example), while higher news density scores than Elena correspond to low or negative news change scores. Were the database for the hurricane domain larger, it would be worthwhile to exclude hurricanes that strike near New York City from the analysis, but with the relatively small data set this is difficult to do while retaining a reasonably large number of cases. In any case, when individual large events are excluded from the analysis, the results are not significantly different from an analysis of the full data set.

While the correlation results may suggest that using the density measure exclusively is a solution to this anomaly, I resist this temptation. Agenda change and density measure two different things. Agenda change measures the extent to which an agenda expanded after a particular event. This measure corresponds with the date of an event, but we cannot say that all the enlargement of the agenda was solely the result of any one particular event. Agenda density measures the extent to which a *particular event* dominates the agenda, regardless of any trend in the size of the agenda. I combine these two measures in a single measure—an index of agenda activity—that is simply the result of multiplying the change and density scores. This variable therefore discounts events that show high density scores but low change scores, or vice versa, thereby giving us a better sense of which events were most important on the agenda. The top events in the news and congressional agenda activity in each domain are depicted in Table A-2.

Defining "Abnormal Occurrences"

The Nuclear Regulatory Commission's definition of an "abnormal occurrence" is provided in Table A-4. This definition is central to the measurement of event seriousness used in chapter 5.

TABLE A-1   Example of Agenda Density and Indices, Hurricanes

Date	Name	Congress. Agenda Change	Congress. Agenda Density	News Change	News Density	Congress. Agenda Activity Index	Media Agenda Activity Index
8/31/85	Elena	3.500	0.500	2.622	0.123	1.750	0.323
9/26/85	Gloria	0.000	0.000	1.377	0.710	0.000	0.978
10/27/85	Juan	0.000	0.000	−0.706	0.191	0.000	−0.135
11/21/85	Kate	0.000	0.000	−0.775	0.289	0.000	−0.224

TABLE A-2A　Congressional and Media Activity, Earthquakes

Date	Name	Congressional Agenda Activity	Date	Name	Media Agenda Activity
2/9/71	San Fernando, CA	4.763	10/17/89	Loma Prieta, CA	3.088
10/17/89	Loma Prieta, CA	4.142	3/27/64	Prince William Sound, AK	1.630
3/27/64	Prince William Sound, AK	4.000	2/9/71	San Fernando, CA	0.250
10/1/87	Whittier, CA	0.586	5/2/83	Central Coalinga, CA	0.133
3/28/75	Pocatello Valley, ID	0.090	1/24/80	Livermore, CA	0.029
5/2/83	Central Coalinga, CA	0.027	8/13/78	California	0.023
10/15/79	California/ Mexico	0.020	10/15/79	California/ Mexico	0.023
1/24/80	Livermore, CA	0.020	11/24/87	Superstition Hills, CA	0.022

TABLE A-2B　Congressional and Media Activity, Hurricanes

Date	Name	Congressional Agenda Activity	Date	Name	Media Agenda Activity
9/6/65	Betsy	61.184	9/21/89	Hugo	2.200
8/17/69	Camille	30.964	9/6/74	Carmen	1.136
6/20/72	Agnes	11.170	9/26/85	Gloria	0.978
10/3/64	Hilda	8.824	9/16/88	Gilbert	0.968
9/21/89	Hugo	1.907	8/9/76	Belle	0.849
8/31/85	Elena	1.750	9/4/79	David	0.789
9/16/88	Gilbert	0.863	8/18/83	Alicia	0.576
9/13/79	Frederic	0.583	8/26/64	Cleo	0.557
8/18/83	Alicia	0.397	8/17/69	Camille	0.412

TABLE A-3 Data Sources and Transformations

Variable	Defined	Source	Transformation[a]
Impact	Interaction term: Damage times deaths.	—	—
Deaths	Number of people killed in the disaster.	Earthquake: USGS database of major seismic event; Hurricane: Herbert and Case, 1990.	Earthquake: Square root. Hurricane: Cube root.
Damage (earthquake and hurricane)	Amount of damage done by event in 1990 dollars.	Earthquake: USGS database of major seismic events; Hurricane: Herbert and Case, 1990.	Earthquake: Square root. Hurricane: Cube root.
Damage (nuclear)	As a measure of seriousness, the number of times that an incident was reported in a follow-up in the NRC's Abnormal Occurrence Reports (AORs)	NRC *Report to Congress on Abnormal Occurrences*	Cube root
Scope	For disasters, the number of people in areas declared disaster areas. For oil spills, the number of people in counties where oil spilled or washed up on shore. For nuclear power, the population of the county in which the nuclear plant in question is sited, and all neighboring counties.	Federal Register, news accounts, Abnormal Occurrence Reports, census data.	Hurricane, Nuclear: Cube Root Earthquake: Square Root Oil Spill: None

continued

TABLE A-3 *Continued*

Variable	Defined	Source	Transformation[a]
Congressional agenda change	Index: Rate of change of testimony in earthquake or hurricane field, two years after event compared to two years before, plus rate of change in bill introductions. This sum is then divided by two.	All Domains: Congressional hearing testimony found through CIS CD-ROM (hereinafter Testimony Database); CCH Legislative Index and Library of Congress information system for bills.	Earthquake, Hurricane, Oil Spill: None. Nuclear: Cube root
Congressional agenda density	Number of witnesses mentioning the current event divided by all testimony for the two years after the disaster (possible range of 0.0 to 1.0).	Testimony database.	Earthquake, Hurricane, Oil Spill: Square root. Nuclear: Cube root
Congressional and news agenda activity	Agenda change times agenda density (agenda density used as a discount factor).	Testimony database and *New York Times Index*.	All: None.
News change	Change in news coverage of earthquakes or hurricanes, two years after event compared with two years before.	*New York Times Index*.	Earthquake, Hurricane, Oil Spill: Square root. Nuclear: Cube root
News density	Extent to which news coverage in field after an event is about the particular event (possible range of 0.0 to 1.0).	*New York Times Index*.	Earthquake: Cube root. Hurricane, Oil Spill: Square root. Nuclear: Cube root

Mobilization	Ratio of representatives of groups that generally support policy change to representatives of groups that oppose change.	Testimony database.	Earthquake, Hurricane, Oil Spill: None. Nuclear: Cube root
Rarity	Span of time since last event of similar magnitude in terms of deaths and damage.	Computed from USGS and Herbert and Case data for Earthquake and Hurricane, Various oil spill data sources; NRC AORs for Nuclear.	Earthquake, Hurricane, Oil Spill: Square root. Nuclear: Cube root
Tone	Extent of support for existing policy or for change in policy. Support for existing policy = +1. Support for change = −1. Neutral = 0. This is mean tone of all participants in two years after event.	Testimony database.	Earthquake, Hurricane, Oil Spill: Square root. Nuclear: Cube root
Policy type	Predominant topic discussed by the witness in a congressional hearing. Type assigned and terminology cross-checked for consistency with types used in other fields.	Testimony database.	N/A
Group type	The type of group represented by the witness. Group type assigned and terminology cross-checked for consistency with types used in other fields.	Testimony database.	N/A

[a]Transformations as required to meet assumptions of OLS regression.

157

TABLE A-4   Nuclear Regulatory Commission Criteria for Abnormal Occurrences

---

An event will be considered an AO [abnormal occurrence] if it involves a major reduction in the degree of protection of the public health or safety. Such an event would involve a moderate or more severe impact on the public health or safety and could include but need not be limited to:

1. Moderate exposure to, or release of, radioactive material licensed by or otherwise regulated by the Commission;
2. Major degradation of essential safety-related equipment; or
3. Major deficiencies in the design, construction, use of, or management controls for licensed facilities or material.

Examples of the types of events that are evaluated in detail using these criteria are:

For Commercial Nuclear Power Plants

1. Exceeding a safety limited of license Technical Specifications [10 CFR 50.36(c)].
2. Major degradation of fuel integrity, primary coolant pressure boundary, or primary containment boundary.
3. Loss of plant capability to perform essential safety functions such that a potential release of radioactivity in excess of 10 CFR Part 100 guidelines could result from a postulated transient or accident (e.g., loss of emergency core cooling system, loss of control rod system).
4. Discovery of a major condition not specifically considered in the Safety Analysis Report (SAR) or Technical Specifications that requires immediate remedial action.
5. Personnel error or procedural deficiencies that result in loss of plant capability to perform essential safety functions such that a potential release of radioactivity in excess of 10 CFR Part 100 guidelines could result from a postulated transient or accident (e.g., loss of emergency core cooling system, loss of control rod system).

Source: Nuclear Regulatory Commission 1994, 15–16.

Notes

CHAPTER 2

1. Of course, a few events are mobilizing even if they only happen ostensibly to one person or victim but are treated as symbolic of what happens to many people. A primary example of such an event is the beating of Rodney King by Los Angeles policy officers. This event was symbolically powerful for many people (often but not always members of racial or ethnic minorities) who had been victims of police brutality in some way. (I thank Regina Lawrence for this insight.) These events are another type of focusing event, which I leave for future studies of this phenomenon.

2. In empirical terms, this means that news coverage is the dependent variable in the first phase, whereupon news coverage, along with other attributes of the event, become independent variables in the second phase.

3. At least, those that I study in this book. Clearly, if a nuclear disaster on the scale of Chernobyl were to occur in the United States, it would have far less ambiguous effects on human populations and on United States politics. However, I confine this study to the agenda-setting power of events that occurred in the United States. This is because events that occur overseas are far less powerful, in agenda setting terms, than domestic events (Smith 1992).

CHAPTER 3

1. Tropical storms also form in the Pacific, and the largest of these are known as cyclones. I do not include Pacific storms in this study.

2. Hurricanes were traditionally given female names until the practice aroused the opposition of some women's groups; the leader of the National Organization for Women suggested that storms be named after male U.S. Senators instead (Krebs 1972, 23:5). The editors of the *Times* suggested, tongue at least partially in cheek, that storm intensity increased after male names were adopted in 1979 (New York Times 1979, IV, 8:2).

3. From this point, I refer to the congressional agenda as the particular subset of the institutional agenda I study in this book. I do so to distinguish the congressional agenda from the institutional agenda, broadly defined, which could include the executive and judicial branches as well.

4. This discussion is drawn primarily from May (1985), especially chapter 2.

5. The construction of the news density variable, and the rationale behind it, is described in greater detail in the methodological appendix.

6. On this point, see Sheets (1995). Bob Sheets, the former director of the National Hurricane Center, explicitly notes the lack of a national hurricane program, and points out that federal spending and research efforts on earthquakes are far greater than similar efforts to deal with hurricanes.

7. It is important to stress that I am not arguing that there is no scientific or political activity at the federal level. Rather, I am arguing that this effort is much smaller than the earthquake program, and does not have the institutional staying power that the NEHRP has. This is due, simply, to the fact that the less-formal Hurricane Program at FEMA is not codified in law and is not formally funded and reauthorized by Congress. Without a program similar to NEHRP, it is unlikely that the hurricane policy community will achieve the cohesiveness needed to attract and hold the attention of interested members of Congress, for the reasons explained in this chapter.

CHAPTER 4

1. For a general discussion of this spill, see Davidson (1990), Keeble (1991), and Wheelwright (1994).

2. In 1979, Alabama, Alaska, California, Connecticut, Florida, Georgia, Louisiana, Maryland, Massachusetts, Mississippi, New Jersey, New York, North Carolina, Oregon, Texas, Virginia, and Washington all had some sort of fund or liability system regarding oil spills; some states included hazardous substances in the legislation. All but six of these states had some sort of cleanup fund, and all but four states provided for unlimited liability for spillers (Mendelsohn and Fidell 1979, 495).

3. The Arctic National Wildlife Refuge (ANWR) is located in northeastern Alaska, near the huge North Slope oil fields. Oil companies have pressed for years to open the refuge for oil exploration and production, while environmental groups have been equally vociferous in their opposition to oil development. The balance of forces on this issue appeared to favor prooil interests until the *Exxon Valdez* spill tilted sentiment against oil companies.

4. A similar argument was made when I met with a senior Alaska state legislator in the summer of 1996. I asked the legislator what was the most important long-term influence of the *Exxon Valdez* spill. I was told that the spill's most important influence was that it evolved into a full funding program for environmentalists, and that the spill was not a disaster because no one was killed.

CHAPTER 5

1. This is an oft-quoted contention used by antinuclear activists to illustrate the naïveté of early proponents of nuclear power. This statement is from Atomic Energy Commission Chairman Lewis L. Strauss, at a 1954 speech before the National Association of Science Writers (Hilgartner, Bell, and O'Connor 1983, 44).

2. The NRC's definition of an "abnormal occurrence" is provided in the appendix.

3. See the appendix for the transformations performed on the variables. These transformations, as in the earlier chapters, were performed so as to provide for more normally distributed variables, an important requirement for OLS estimation. However, no reasonable transformations could mask the outlying nature of the TMI case on most variables. One effect of extreme outliers is to inflate the R^2 of the model, which seems to appear in Table 5-1. I thus report two results that include and exclude the TMI case to reveal the influence of the outlier. This is a standard method of clarifying this effect (Bornstedt and Knoke 1988, 289).

4. These were hearings that were held by the AEC to determine the need for additional core cooling systems at existing and proposed nuclear plants. Concerns had been raised that existing cooling systems and their backups were inadequate in the event of an accident.

5. A reactor-year is the equivalent of one nuclear plant running for one year.

6. This account is a summary of the account of this accident in Perrow 1984, 50-54.

7. A scram is an unplanned shutdown of a nuclear reactor. The term "scram" dates from the early days of nuclear reactors. It is said that, if a nuclear plant starts running out of control, one should seek to control the reaction (using the carbon control rods, for example, to slow the chain reaction) and then one should "scram" if the reactor remained critical. Automatic scrams are usually the result of properly working safety systems. Unplanned and manual scrams, as at Fermi, are considerably more difficult to manage and are therefore more dangerous.

8. So called because it was said, somewhat facetiously, that if the containment failed, and the core melted through the floor, the hot material would melt a hole in the earth all the way to China.

CHAPTER 6

1. Perrow (1984, 263) notes that one reason for the complexity and cost of manned spaceflight, as opposed to unmanned probes, was the need to create safety systems and backup systems to those systems, simply to keep the astronauts alive through the flight. Such systems add greater complexity to the system, rendering them potentially more dangerous.

References

Anderson, James E. 1994. *Public Policymaking: An Introduction.* 2nd ed. Boston: Houghton Mifflin.

Baumgartner, Frank, and Bryan D. Jones. 1993. *Agendas and Instability in American Politics.* Chicago: University of Chicago Press.

Bennett, Colin J., and Michael Howlett. 1992. "The Lessons of Learning: Reconciling Theories of Policy Learning and Policy Change." *Policy Sciences* 25 (3):275–294.

Bennett, W. Lance. 1995. *News, The Politics of Illusion.* 3rd ed. New York: Longman.

Bookchin, Murray. 1989. "Death of a Small Planet: It's Growth That's Killing Us." *The Progressive* 53 (August):19–23.

Bornstedt, George W., and David Knoke. 1988. *Statistics for Social Data Analysis.* 2nd ed. Ithaca, Ill.: F.E. Peacock.

Burby, Raymond J., and Linda C. Dalton. 1993. "State Planning Mandates and Coastal Management." In *Coastal Zone '93,* edited by W. S. W. Orville T. Magoon, Hugh Converse and L. Tomas Tobin. New York: American Society of Civil Engineers.

Burnier, DeLysa. 1994. "Constructing Political Reality: Language, Symbols, and Meaning in Politics: A Review Essay." *Political Research Quarterly* 47 (1):239–253.

Burstein, Paul. 1991. "Policy Domains: Organization, Culture, and Policy Outcomes." *Annual Review of Sociology* 17:327–50.

Cable, Sherry, and Charles Cable. 1995. *Environmental Problems, Grassroots Solutions: The Politics of Grassroots Environmental Conflict:* New York: St. Martin's.

Carmines, Edward G., and James A. Stimson. 1989. *Issue Evolution: Race and the Transformation of American Politics.* Princeton: Princeton University Press.

Carson, Rachel. 1962. *Silent Spring.* Greenwich, Conn.: Fawcett.

Clarfield, Gerald H., and William M. Weicek. 1984. *Nuclear America: Military and Civilian Nuclear Power in the United States, 1940–1980.* New York: St. Martin's Press.

Cobb, Roger, Jeannie-Keith Ross, and Marc Howard Ross. 1976. "Agenda Building as a Comparative Political Process." *American Political Science Review* 70 (1):126–138.

Cobb, Roger W., and Charles D. Elder. 1983. *Participation in American Politics: The Dynamics of Agenda-Building.* 2nd ed. Baltimore: Johns Hopkins University Press.

Cochran, Clarke E., Lawrence Mayer, T. R. Carr, and N. Joseph Cayer. 1986. *American Public Policy*. 2nd ed. New York: St. Martin's Press.

Comey, David Dinsmore. 1979. "The Browns Ferry Incident." In *Accidents Will Happen: The Case Against Nuclear Power*, edited by L. Stephenson and G. R. Zachar. New York: Perennial Library/Harper and Row.

Congressional Quarterly. 1972. "Alaska Pipeline: Back to Court Despite Interior's OK." *Congressional Quarterly Almanac* 28:564–568.

Congressional Quarterly. 1975. "Nuclear Insurance Program." *Congressional Quarterly Almanac* 31:276–279.

Congressional Quarterly. 1977a. "Energy Research Funds Vetoed." *Congressional Quarterly Almanac* 33:683–691.

Congressional Quarterly. 1977b. "Oil Pollution Bills Considered." *Congressional Quarterly Almanac* 33:668–670.

Congressional Quarterly. 1979. "Nuclear Power Legislation Fails to Clear." *Congressional Quarterly Almanac* 35:693–699.

Congressional Quarterly. 1989a. "ANWR Oil Drilling Bill Goes Nowhere in 1989." *Congressional Quarterly Almanac* 45:678.

Congressional Quarterly. 1989b. "Approval of Liability Bills Spurred by Alaska Spill." *Congressional Quarterly Almanac* 45:682–87.

Davidson, Art. 1990. *In the Wake of the Exxon Valdez*. San Francisco: Sierra Club Books.

Davidson, Roger H., and Walter J. Oleszek. 1994. *Congress and Its Members*. Washington: CQ Press.

Del Sesto, Steven L. 1980. "Conflicting Ideologies of Nuclear Power: Congressional Testimony on Nuclear Power." *Public Policy* 28 (1):39–70.

Devanney, J.W., S. Protopapa, and R. Klock. 1989. *Tanker Spills, Collisions, and Groundings*. Cambridge, Mass.: Sea Grant College Program, MIT.

Downs, Anthony. 1972. "Up and Down with Ecology: The Issue Attention Cycle." *The Public Interest* 28 (Summer):38–50.

Dunlap, Riley E., and Angela G. Mertig. 1992. "The Evolution of the U.S. Environmental Movement from 1970 to 1990: An Overview." In *American Environmentalism: The U.S. Environmental Movement, 1970–1990*, edited by R. E. Dunlap and A. G. Mertig. New York: Taylor and Francis.

Dye, Thomas R. 1992. *Understanding Public Policy*. 7th ed. Englewood Cliffs, N.J.: Prentice-Hall.

Easton, Robert Olney. 1972. *Black Tide: The Santa Barbara Oil Spill and its Consequences*. New York: Delacorte.

Edelman, Murray J. 1967. *The Symbolic Uses of Politics*. Urbana: University of Illinois Press.

Edelman, Murray J. 1988. *Constructing the Political Spectacle*. Chicago: University of Chicago Press.

Epstein, Edward J. 1973. *News From Nowhere: Television and the News*. New York: Random House.

Federal Emergency Management Agency. 1992. *Building for the Future: National Eathquake Hazards Reduction Program, Fiscal Years 1991–1992 Report to Congress*. Washington: Federal Emergency Management Agency.

Fischoff, Baruch, Paul Slovic, and Sarah Lichtenstein. 1979a. "Images of Disaster: Perception and Acceptance of Risks from Nuclear Power." In *Energy Risk Management*, edited by G. Goodman and W. D. Rowe. New York: Academic Press.

Fischoff, Baruch, Paul Slovic, and Sarah Lichtenstein. 1979b. "Weighing the Risks." *Environment* 21 (1):17–38.

Fricke, Peter, and John Maiolo. 1978. *A Study of Public Knowledge and Perception of the Effects of the "Argo Merchant" Oil Spill*. Institute for Coastal and Marine Resoruces Technical Report No. 3.

Gallagher, John. 1990. "In the Wake of the Exxon Valdez: Murky Legal Waters of Liability and Compensation." *New England Law Review* 25:571–616.

Gamson, W. A., and A. Modigliani. 1989. "Media Discourse and Public Opinion on Nuclear Power." *American Journal of Sociology* (95):1–37.

Gates, George O. 1972. *The San Fernando Earthquake of February 9, 1971, and Public Policy*. Sacramento: California Legislature.

Gaventa, John. 1980. *Power and Powerlessness: Quiescence and Rebellion in an Appalachian Valley*. Urbana: University of Illinois Press.

Greenberg, George D., Jeffrey A. Miller, Lawrence B. Mohr, and Bruce C. Vladeck. 1977. "Developing Public Policy Theory: Perspectives from Emperical Research." *American Political Science Review* 71 (4):1532–1543.

Gusfield, Joseph. 1981. *The Culture of Public Problems: Drinking Driving and the Symbolic Order*. Chicago: University of Chicago Press.

Hilgartner, James, and Charles Bosk. 1988. "The Rise and Fall of Social Problems: A Public Arenas Model." *American Journal of Sociology* 94 (1):53–78.

Hilgartner, Stephen, Richard C. Bell, and Rory O'Connor. 1983. *Nukespeak: The Selling of Nuclear Technology in America*. New York: Penguin.

Housner, George M. 1994. *The Continuing Challenge: The Northridge Earthquake of January 17, 1994*. Sacramento, Calif.: California Department of Transportation.

Ingram, Helen, and Dean Mann. 1980. "Policy Failure: An Issue Deserving Attention." In *Why Policies Succeed or Fail*, edited by H. Ingram and D. Mann. Beverly Hills: Sage.

Interagency Committee on Ocean Pollution Research, Development & Marketing. 1981. *National Marine Pollution Program Plan*. Washington: The Committee.

Jasper, James M. 1988. "The Political Life-Cycle of Technological Controversies." *Social Forces* 67 (2):357–377.

Jones, Walter. 1989. "Oil Spill Compensation and Liability Legislation: When Good Things Don't Happen to Good Bills." *Environmental Law Reporter* 10:10333–10335.

Joppke, Christian. 1993. *Mobilizing Against Nuclear Energy: A Comparison of Germany and the United States*. Berkeley: University of California Press.

Keeble, John. 1991. *Out of the Channel*. New York: Harper Collins.

Kemp, Kathleen. 1984. "Accidents, Scandals, and Political Support for Regulatory Agencies." *Journal of Politics* 46 (2):401–427.

Kifner, John. 1976. "Key Tanker Gear Turned Off, U.S. Aides Say." *New York Times*, December 24, A1:1.

Kim, J. K., P. Shaor-Ghaffari, and J. J. Gustainis. 1990. "Agenda-Setting Functions of a Mass Event: the Case of 'Amerika'." *Political Communication and Persuasion* 7:1–10.

Kingdon, John W. 1995. *Agendas, Alternatives and Public Policies*. 2nd ed. New York: Harper Collins.

Knoke, David, and Edward O. Laumann. 1982. "The Social Organization of National Policy Domains: An Exploration of Some Structural Hypotheses." In *Social Structure and Network Analysis*, edited by P. V. Marsden and N. Lin. Beverly Hills: Sage.

Krebs, Albin. 1972. "Notes on People." *New York Times*, January 21, 23:5.

Laumann, Edward O., and David Knoke. 1987. *The Organizational State: Social Choice in National Policy Domains*. Madison: University of Wisconsin Press.

Light, Paul C. 1982. *The President's Agenda: Domestic Policy Choice from Kennedy to Carter (with Notes on Ronald Reagan)*. Baltimore: Johns Hopkins University Press.

Lindblom, Charles E. 1959. "The Science of 'Muddling Through'." *Public Administration Review* 19:79–88.

Lindblom, Charles. 1979. "Still Muddling, Not Yet Through." *Public Administration Review* 39:517–526.

Lovins, Amory B., and L. Hunter Lovins. 1980. *Energy/War: Breaking the Nuclear Link*. San Francisco: Friends of the Earth.

Majone, Giandomenico. 1989. *Evidence, Argument and Persuasion in the Policy Process*. New Haven: Yale University Press.

May, Peter J. 1985. *Recovering from Catastrophes: Federal Disaster Relief Policy and Politics*. Westport, Conn.: Greenwood Press.

May, Peter J. 1990. "Reconsidering Policy Design: Policies and Publics." *Journal of Public Policy* 11 (2):187–206.

May, Peter J. 1992. "Policy Learning and Failure." *Journal of Public Policy* 12 (4):331–354.

May, Peter J., and Thomas A. Birkland. 1994. "Earthquake Risk Reduction: An Examination of Local Regulatory Efforts." *Environmental Management* 18 (6):923–939.

McCann, Michael W. 1986. *Taking Reform Seriously*. Ithaca, NY: Cornell University Press.

Mendelsohn, Allen I., and Eugene R. Fidell. 1979. "Liability for Oil Pollution—United States Law." *Journal of Maritime Law and Commerce* 10 (4):475–496.

Mitchell, Robert Cameron, Angela G. Mertig, and Riley E. Dunlap. 1992. "Twenty Years of Environmental Mobilization: Trends Among National Environmental Organizations." In *American Environmentalism: The U.S. Environmental Movement, 1970–1990*, edited by R. E. Dunlap and A. G. Mertig. New York: Taylor and Francis.

Molotch, Harvey. 1970. "Santa Barbara: Oil in the Velvet Playground." In *Eco-Catastrophe*. New York: Harper and Row.

Molotch, Harvey, and Marilyn Lester. 1975. "Accidental News: The Great Oil Spill as Local Occurrence and National Event." *American Journal of Sociology* 81 (2):235–261.

Morgan, M. Granger. 1993. "Risk Analysis and Management." *Scientific American* 269 (1):32–41.

Nader, Ralph. 1979. "Introduction." In *Accidents Will Happen: The Case Against Nuclear Power*, edited by L. Stephenson and G. R. Zachar. New York: Perennial Library/Harper and Row.

Nash, A. E. Keir, Dean E. Mann, and Phil G. Olson. 1972. *Oil Pollution and the Public Interest: A Study of the Santa Barbara Oil Spill*. Berkeley: Institute of Governmental Studies, University of California.

National Research Council, Commission on Geosciences, Environment and Resources, U.S. National Committee for the Decade for Natural Disaster Reduction. 1991. *A Safer Future: Reducing the Impacts of Natural Disasters.* Washington: National Academy Press.

National Response Team. 1989. *The Exxon Valdez Oil Spill.* [Washington: The Response Team].

Nelkin, Dorothy. 1981. "Some Social and Political Dimensions of Nuclear Power: Examples from Three Mile Island." *American Political Science Review* 75 (1):132–145.

New York Times. 1976. "Plan to Burn Spilled Oil is Rejected." *New York Times,* December 25, A1:5.

New York Times. 1979. "Brotherly Storm." *New York Times,* September 9, A18:2.

New York Times. 1994. "Whitman Signs Bill to Protect Pipeline." *New York Times,* October 20, B6.

Nuclear Regulatory Commission. 1994. *Report to Congress on Abnormal Occurrences.* Vol. 17 no. 2. Washington, D.C.: Government Printing Office.

O'Toole, Laurence J. 1989. The Public Administrator's Role in Setting the Policy Agenda. In *Handbook of Public Administration*, edited by J. L. Perry. San Francisco: Jossey Bass.

Perrow, Charles. 1984. *Normal Accidents: Living with High-Risk Technologies.* New York: Basic Books.

Peters, B. Guy. 1993. *American Public Policy: Promise and Performance.* Chatham, N.J.: Chatham House.

Potter, Jeffrey. 1973. *Disaster By Oil.* New York: Macmillan.

Randle, Russell V. 1991. "The Oil Pollution Act of 1990: Its Provisions, Intent and Effects." *Environmental Law Reporter* 21 (10119–10135).

Ripley, Randall, and Grace Franklin. 1984. *Congress, the Bureaucracy and Public Policy.* 3rd ed. Homewood, Ill.: Dorsey Press.

Rogers, Everett M., James W. Dearing, and Dorine Bergman. 1992. "The Anatomy of Agenda-Setting Research." Unpublished manuscript.

Rogers, Everett M., James W. Dearing, and Wen-Ying Liu. 1992. "Looking Backward and Looking Forward at Approaches to Agenda-Setting Research." Paper read at American Political Science Association.

Rosenbaum, Walter A. 1991. *Environmental Politics and Policy.* 2nd ed. Washington: Congressional Quarterly Press.

Rossi, Peter H., James D. Wright, and Eleanor Weber-Burdin. 1982. *Natural Hazards and Public Choice: The State and Local Politics of Hazard Mitigation.* New York: Academic Press.

Sabatier, Paul A. 1988. "An Advocacy Coalition Framework of Policy Change and the Role of Policy-Oriented Learning Therein." *Policy Sciences* 21:129–168.

Sabatier, Paul A. 1991. "Political Science and Public Policy." *PS: Political Science and Politics* 24 (2):144–156.

Satchell, Michael, and Betsey Carpenter. 1989. "A Disaster that Wasn't." *U.S. News and World Report* (Sept. 18):61–69.

Schattschneider, E.E. 1960/1975. *The Semisovereign People.* Hinsdale, Ill.: The Dryden Press.

Schneider, Anne, and Helen Ingram. 1993. "The Social Construction of Target Populations: Implications for Politics and Policy." *American Political Science Review* 87 (2):334–348.

Sheets, Robert C. 1995. "Stormy Weather." *Forum Applied Research and Public Policy* 10 (Spring):5–15.

Slater, Dashka. 1994. "Dress Rehearsal for Disaster." *Sierra* 79 (3):53–57.

Slovic, Paul, Sarah Lichtenstein, and Baruch Fischoff. 1984. "Modeling the Societal Risks of Fatal Accidents." *Management Science* 30 (4):464–474.

Smith, Conrad. 1991. "News Sources and Power Elites in Newspaper Coverage of the Exxon Valdez Oil Spill." Paper read at Association for Education in Journalism and Mass Communication, at Boston.

Smith, Conrad. 1992. *Media and Apocalypse: News Coverage of the Yellowstone Forest Fires, Exxon Valdez Oil Spill, and Loma Prieta Earthqauke.* Westport, Conn.: Greenwood Press.

Smith, Steven S., and Christopher J. Deering. 1984. *Committees in Congress.* Washington: Congressional Quarterly Press.

Stallings, Robert A. 1995. *Promoting Risk: Constructing the Earthquake Threat.* New York: DeGruyter.

Steinhart, John, and Carol Steinhart. 1972. *Blowout: A Case Study of the Santa Barbara Oil Spill.* Belmont, Calif.: Wadsworth.

Stone, Deborah A. 1989. "Causal Stories and the Formation of Policy Agendas." *Political Science Quarterly* 104 (2):281–300.

Sylves, Richard T. 1980. "Carter Nuclear Licensing Reform Versus Three Mile Island." *Publius* 10 (1):69–79.

Temples, James R. 1980. "The Politics of Nuclear Power: A Subgovernment in Transition." *Political Science Quarterly* 95 (Summer):239–260.

United States Department of Commerce, Bureau of the Census. 1993. *Statistical Abstract of the United States.* Washington, D.C.: Government Printing Office.

Vaden, Ted. 1977. "Oil Tanker Accidents." *Congressional Quarterly Weekly Report* 35 (Jan. 15):82–83.

Walker, Jack L. 1977. "Setting the Agenda in the U.S. Senate: A Theory of Problem Selection." *British Journal of Political Science* 7:423–445.

Wehr, Elizabeth. 1977. "Earthquake Research: A New Emphasis." *Congressional Quarterly Weekly Report* 35 (28 [July 9]):1412–13.

Weingast, Barry R. 1980. "Congress, Regulation and the Decline of Nuclear Power." *Public Policy* 28 (2):231–255.

Weiss, Ellyn R. 1979. "Three Mile Island: The Loss of Innocence." In *Accidents Will Happen: The Case Against Nuclear Power*, edited by L. Stephenson and G. R. Zachar. New York: Perennial Library/Harper and Row.

Wheelwright, Jeff. 1994. *Degrees of Disaster: Prince William Sound: How Nature Reels and Rebounds*. New York: Simon and Schuster.

Williams, David E., and Glenda Treadaway. 1992. "Exxon and The Valdez Accident: A Failure in Crisis Communication." *Communication Studies* 43 (Spring):56–64.

Zahariadis, Nikolaos. 1993. "To Sell or Not to Sell? Telecommunications Policy in Britain and France." *Journal of Public Policy* 12 (4):355–376.

Index

nuclear power accidents, *continued*
  issue containment of, 123–124
  political polarization in, 40,
    117, 122–123, 128, 130
  public participation in policy
    making in, 42
  symbols of, 12
  Three Mile Island (TMI), 1979,
    12, 19, 28, 107–108, 109, 110
    and *The China Syndrome*,
      127–128
    distinguished from Fermi
      and Browns Ferry, 127
    as "incident" or
      "accident," 143
    as mobilizing event, 122
    policy change and,
      139–140, 142, 143
    windows of opportunity
      and, 116, 140
Nuclear Regulatory Commission, 28
nuclear weapons, 5

Oil Pollution Act (1990), 3, 28, 40,
  85, 137, 141
  deadlock over, 74, 83
  double-hull tankers and, 78
  Exxon Valdez spill and, 40, 74,
    85, 104
oil spill policy, 74–105
  cargo preferences and, 82
  Clean Water Act and, 81
  cleanup responsibility, 83
  Comprehensive Environmental
    Response, Condensation,
    and Liability Act
    (Superfund), 83
  confounded with other issues,
    82–83
  deadlock over, 74, 83–84, 103
  Deepwater Port Act (DWPA)
    and, 81, 82
  as disjointed policy, 80–83
  federalism and, 80
  hazardous materials and, 80,
    83

liability and, 83
Limitation of Liability Act
  and, 80–81
Mitchell, George (Senator)
  and, 84
Muskie, Edmund (Senator)
  and, 83
Outer Continental Shelf Lands
  Act Amendments and,
  81–82
polarized policy in, 40
preemption of federal policy
  by states and, 80, 83–85,
  102–103
private sector and, 77–78
public participation in, 42
Superfund and, 83
Tanker Safety Act and, 82
tanker safety and, 82
Trans Alaska Pipeline
  Authorization Act
  (TAPAA) and, 81, 82, 103
unification of, 82–83
oil spills, 19, 74–105
  advocacy coalitions and, 78
  as ambiguous in their effects,
    43
  Argo Merchant (1976), 74, 100,
    101, 102, 103, 141
  as environmental harms, 44
  Exxon Valdez (1989), 3–4,
    12–13, 91–92, 94
  group mobilization and, 93–97
  Hickel, Walter, and, 101
  issue containment and, 89–93
  liability for, 80–82, 102–104
  Olympic Games (1976), 100–104
  policy outcomes from, 100–104
  Santa Barbara (1969), 2, 4,
    76–77, 79, 90–91, 93
  as "situation" during WW II,
    75
  social construction and, 89–93
  symbols of, 33, 97–100
  triggering legislation, 3–4
  volume of, and actual harm,
    44, 86

CPSIA information can be obtained at www.ICGtesting.com
Printed in the USA
BVOW01s2344230315

392996BV00001B/35/P